TRIAD POWER

TRIAD POWER

The Coming Shape
of Global Competition

KENICHI OHMAE

THE FREE PRESS
A Division of Macmillan, Inc.
NEW YORK

Collier Macmillan Publishers
LONDON

The Free Press
A Division of Macmillan, Inc.
866 Third Avenue, New York, N.Y. 10022

Collier Macmillan Canada, Inc.

Printed in the United States of America

printing number
1 2 3 4 5 6 7 8 9 10

Library of Congress Cataloging in Publication Data

Ohmae, Kenichi.
  Triad power.

  Includes index.
  1. Joint ventures. 2. International business enterprises. 3. Competition, international. I. Title.
HD62.47.036 1985   338.8′8   84–26068
ISBN 0–02–923470–0

*To my fellow partners
at McKinsey & Company*

ACKNOWLEDGMENTS

THE OLD MODEL of the multinational enterprise has become obsolete. But what is the right model to use? I have been thinking about this question for a long time. At the outset I was particularly influenced by John Tomb, who opened McKinsey & Company's Tokyo office in 1971 and was a leading advocate of the "evolution theory" of multinationals. I was also greatly influenced by Gilbert Clee, a respected senior partner of McKinsey and our managing director at the time of his death in 1971. Clee introduced the term "global enterprise" in his *Harvard Business Review* article in 1959, describing the homogeneous world market and encouraging American companies to buy low-cost raw materials anywhere in the world, produce in countries with low labor costs, and sell in attractive markets. His model was based on the global optimization concept. As time went by and I accumulated more experience working with major corporations in Japan, the United States, Europe, and more recently in Southeast Asia, I came to realize that none of the models, including Clee's, fitted reality. Nor did they point the way for reshaping corporations during the post–energy crisis era.

During the late 1970s and early 1980s, I began sketching

out my own view and sharing it with my colleagues at McKinsey. With their encouragement, I started a small internal project to fully develop this view, initially with my Tokyo colleagues Yoshinori Yokoyama and Ryuji Yasuda, and subsequently with Herbert Henzler in Munich and Charles Farr in New York. There is frequent mention of the Triad throughout the book. With the formation of our Japan–European Community–United States "syndicate," we made up such a Triad, developed a data base, and exchanged perspectives. During the initial phase of the project, we were joined by Fred Hilmer of Australia and Sigurd Reinton from the United Kingdom, both of whom are important cosmopolitan members of our firm. Subsequently, Tino Puri of our New York office has joined this internal group, and with his leadership, the project has become an ongoing effort at McKinsey. My predecessors as manager of McKinsey's Tokyo office, Quincy Hunsicker (now in Zurich) and James Balloun (now in Atlanta), have continued to provide stimulating perspective on multinational corporations, particularly with respect to Japan, their second home.

When I was a member of McKinsey's Executive Committee it was like sitting right in the Triad. Max Geldens and Mickey Huibregtsen come from Europe. Fred Gluck and Mike Bulkin bring their American perspective. Our managing director, Ron Daniel, continually visits our 33 offices around the world and is, I believe, the closest incarnation of the global perspective I espouse in this book. I want to express my sincere thanks to these colleagues. In our frequent and heated discussions, they always drag me out of Japan to those corners of the world where I cannot help but be reminded of the whole world. From outside Japan, I can see the picture much more clearly and have a perspective I could not have achieved if my experience had been limited to eating *sashimi* and *sushi* in Tokyo.

I would also like to thank the many people who helped me in preparing the data, clippings, and analyses, and in editing and proofreading the manuscript. Tomoko Okayasu produced the original typescript under the supervision of Taeko Sugeno. Kiyoko Koshimizu, my secretary, handled the correspondence and clippings. Norma Chaty and Sue Bruser helped me with their editing in Tokyo, and Bill Price supervised the editing and production at McKinsey in New York, with the help of Edith Lewis at The Free Press. My thanks to Joseph Pomerance for his meticulous copyediting. I am grateful to Bob Wallace of The Free Press for his consideration and enthusiasm. Ever since Bob first expressed his keen interest in my previous book, *The Mind of the Strategist,* he has encouraged me to complete this present work.

Finally, I thank the clients, partners, and staff members of that truly multinational firm, McKinsey & Company. Even though the point of view I argue for in *Triad Power* is entirely mine, my work and my colleagues at McKinsey have had great influence on my thinking.

CONTENTS

CONTENTS

Part IV. Becoming a Triad Power

PREFACE

NOW THAT WE have awakened from the nightmare of the 1973 energy crisis, we have discovered that the pace of technological changes has not only accelerated once again but has in fact exploded. We have seen, too, that the developed nations have become very similar in terms of their sociopolitical behavior.

With Japan's emergence as an industrial power, the combined gross national product (GNP) of Japan and the United States alone accounts for 30 percent of the Free World's total. If the four key countries of the European Community, that is, the United Kingdom, West Germany, France, and Italy, are added to this, the figure reaches 45 percent. In fact, the Organization for Economic Cooperation and Development (OECD) nations, which make up only 15 percent of the total number of countries in the world, account for as much as 54 percent of the global GNP. These countries have very similar problems: a mature and stagnant economy, escalating social costs, an aging population, lack of jobs for skilled workers, and at the same time, dynamic technological developments coupled with the ever-escalating costs of research and development (R&D) and modern production facilities.

Global enterprises that established their modus operandi mainly in the 1960s now are faced with discrepancies between their traditional approach and these new realities. They are out of date. Each age has a form of business organization appropriate to the tempo of its times.

In the field of consumer goods, Unilever (British–Dutch), one of the world's oldest and largest multinational corporations, reflects the colonization period of European dominance. European enterprises such as Philips of the Netherlands have organized each of their businesses around the world to run as independent entities serving the national market where they are situated. Enterprises that operate on this basis usually get their strengths from their strong trade name (for example, Kraft, Nestle, Kellogg, Coca-Cola, and Pepsi-Cola).

Most American multinationals were shaped in the relatively stable era between the two world wars. The underlying philosophy at this time was that the narrow confines of nationality were outmoded and that great corporate wealth would be amassed by doing business with the world as a single, multinational unit.

Some of the unique circumstances of the post–World War II period favored American companies. The nearly prostrate condition of most European and Japanese industrial firms disqualified them from the technological race. U.S. corporations straddled Latin America, Asia, and Europe, inside and outside the European Community (EC) (apparently unaffected by the political and economic division that seems fundamental to the European psyche) and were organized around the fundamental concept that their technological and competitive edge was virtually unassailable. During the first 20 years of the postwar period, for example, some 2,800 U.S. businesses that had a technological advantage (IBM, Texas Instruments, Xerox), a unique product (Gillette, Kellogg), or a leading position in U.S. industry [International Telephone and Telegraph Corporation (ITT), General Motors] had stakes in 10,000 direct investments abroad.

By and large, subsidiaries were formed along a "clone" model—producing and selling substantially the same products as the parent company and operating miniature versions of headquarters organizations. The degree of centralization varied, of course, but home country absolutism was the predominant structural mode in industry operations abroad.

Today, all these conditions have altered dramatically. Disparities of size and technical capabilities between American multinationals and their European and Japanese competitors have narrowed or disappeared. In fact, if the sizes of the American corporations were adjusted for their disproportionately larger domestic market, most American multinationals would be equal in size to their Japanese and European counterparts. And the view of the world as a single, homogeneous economic unit no longer holds. Yet, many of today's leading enterprises are still structured around the traditional feudal, absolute, or multinational models.

My own premise challenges the one-world concept and orthodox nationalism. It focuses on cross-cultural alliances and accepts a future in which change is inevitable and in which there is no reward without risk.

Obviously, the most difficult challenge one faces in such an attempt is to overcome misperceptions. In many cases, today's perception is the product of yesterday's truths, or at least half-truths. This is the reason why we tend to dwell on the currently accepted notion for too long. However, in the realistic world of business, such a tendency clearly weakens a corporation's position relative to both domestic and global competitors. In business a manager's oversight is reflected on the profit and loss statement and balance sheet, rather than in the company's glossy annual report.

I travel out of Japan as much as two dozen times per year. On average, I visit the United States 9 to 12 times a year, Europe at least 2 to 3 times, and Southeast Asia a dozen times. This adds up to, a lot of tiring traveling. On the other hand, the advantage of moving around is that I develop a feel for what's happening around the world, as opposed to reading scholastic doctrines and analyses of global business and the fate of the multinationals. For some time, particularly through working out of Tokyo both for large Japanese companies in the process of becoming global, and for American and European corporations aiming at increasing their business in Japan, I have come to realize that their perception itself is the biggest hindrance that prevents companies from taking advantage of the dynamic and lucrative international marketplace, particularly in, but not limited to, the OECD.

What I mean by perception will be elaborated in the book, but let me try to succinctly state three or four new points of view which illustrate the kind of business world in which we live (or, at least, that world as I see it).

1. Chasing low-labor-cost locations for siting is still in fashion. However, many of these overseas locations are short-lived in terms of their economic competitiveness. Most competitive Japanese companies are pulling out of Southeast Asia and investing in robots and machines.

2. The traditional mode of operation for a prestigious multinational has been to develop an unchallengeable technology, and exploit its potential on its own or through licensing throughout the world. However, three things have happened:

    a. The cost of R&D to come up with any sellable technology has become very high.

    b. Quite a few companies in the OECD possess similar technological competence, and monopoly of any technology has become difficult.

    c. Diffusion of a new technology to, and its acceptance by, various OECD countries has become very fast— from almost a decade to a year.

The combined impact of these three factors calls for a company's ability to penetrate into major countries of the OECD almost simultaneously and spontaneously. Failing that, it will have to make arrangements with another company to effectively achieve such an objective, at the same time guarding against a sudden attack by untraditional competitors.

3. There is an emergence of the Triadians, or the residents of Japan, America, and the European Community. We may call them Triadians, or OECDites. These are the people whose academic backgrounds, income levels (both discretion-

ary and nondiscretionary), life-style, use of leisure time, and aspirations are quite similar. In these democratic countries, the national infrastructure, in terms of highways, telephone systems, sewage disposal, power transmission, and governmental systems, is also very similar. From a corporation's point of view, their basic demand patterns enable them to treat this group of people, some 600 million residents, as belonging to virtually the same species. In fact, the behavior of their younger generation is so similar across the national boundaries (and they all behave like California youngsters—we may term this the "Californianization" of the Free World) that the older generation has difficulty communicating with them. In other words, there is more vertical "generation gap" than horizontal "international gap."

4. Despite consumers' loss of national identity in each of the OECD countries, the protectionist pressures are mounting. Average consumers want the best and the cheapest, regardless of the origin of the products. But the governmental and "expressed" public opinions are pushing the whole world toward the bloc economy. This necessitates that any global enterprise must become a true insider, or honorary citizen, in each of the Triad regions.

These four points are discussed in detail in Part I of this book, entitled "Forces of Change."

In Part II, I try to highlight the "Realities of Global Competition": despite the glorious success stories of the multinationals in every corner of the world, it has become increasingly difficult to repeat the performance of the early pioneers who knocked out the competition and established an enviable position in any country they entered. Mainly due to the aforementioned protectionist forces at work, today even the most powerful and dominant companies headquartered in any of the Triad regions are having difficulty reproducing their performance abroad, especially in the key countries of Japan, America, and the European Community—a phenomenon of impasse.

A company is more likely to be wiped out by its domestic competitors, rather than a "foreign invasion," due mainly to the foreign firms' inability to establish truly profitable and lasting interfaces with the local customers.

In Part III, I describe the most recent diagnostic results of how the Japanese are doing overseas and how the Western corporations are doing in Japan—in other words, the scorecard of the global business game, again drastically different from the general perception. For example:

△ Most Japanese companies, which have been so successful in the past based on exports out of the highly favorable home ground, are now faced with major problems of running full-size and fully integrated operations in the United States and Europe. Their much-praised management system is faced with cultural challenges of transferability, and success so far has been limited to a handful of truly cautious and thorough companies operating in developing countries.

△ Despite the loud public complaints that Japan is closed to foreign businesses, many American and European companies have established a dominant position in Japan. Most of these companies have become true insiders participating with the full spectrum of the Japanese business system, and thus have removed themselves from the "trade statistics" of imports and exports. As they produce and sell in Japan, they have become less visible to Western eyes. Nonetheless, these companies have several points in common, regardless of their industry of specialization, and give us an insight into the successful "insiderization" of a global corporation.

In Part IV, I will expand on the theme of "Becoming a Triad Power":

△ There are three ways to establish a de facto insider position in each Triad region. Of the three options, I submit that the consortium formation is the most realistic and productive. The biggest challenge here is to learn and master the language of communication between two corporations that are in partnership.

△ The real Triad power actually has equally strong holds in the developing regions immediately south of its geographical region. As a result, a Japanese Triad power is operative primarily in the United States, the European Community, and Southeast Asia. With Japan at the center in its mindset, therefore, the Triad actually becomes a Tetrahedron. Likewise, the American Triad includes the United States, Japan, the European Community, and Latin America, and the European Triad consists of Europe, the United States, Japan, and Africa and/or the Middle East. For all of these Triad powers, it is essential that they become truly accepted by, and informed of, these tetrahedral regions (including of course the home region): other regions become less important for survival, and can be treated as marginal and/or opportunistic. Shortcomings of the traditional models, particularly the "United Nations model" of the multinational corporations, have been that they have neglected the significance of these regions and have treated the world as if it consisted of 150 equally important markets.

△ Finally, in order to succeed as a stable Triad power, the viewpoint of a company's headquarters' organization must change, in order to be able to see the critical marketplace at an equidistance regardless of actual physical distance. I call this the "Anchorage perspective," or equidistance (that is, seven hours) to Tokyo, New York, and Dusseldorf from Anchorage, Alaska.

These are my observations. In what follows, I will elaborate on each of these points, and offer my ideas as to how to implement the Triad concept to reap rewards with minimum risks.

While I do not claim academic perfection, I do want to emphasize the importance of these new perspectives for corporations pursuing business around the world. They have been

developed over time as embryonic bits and pieces of hypotheses as I move around the world and talk with various business
and political figures. However, when I come home, I do verify
these hypotheses with analyses based on the data and information available to our Research Department. To the extent that
this is possible, I have tried to share a few of these analyses
with the readers of this book.

PART I

FORCES OF CHANGE

THE SIGNALS OF ECONOMIC DISLOCATION are clearly visible. Zigzagging interest rates, fluctuating currencies, plummeting employment, volatile oil prices, and explosive trade tensions plague the world. The causes? Some allege high-cost labor is the culprit, others single out deficiencies in corporate management, and still others blame government monetary, fiscal, or industrial policies, or the lack of them. Some Westerners blame high taxes, while some accuse the Japanese. Some nationalists claim the fault lies with foreign investments that rob their own citizens of work. Others accuse foreign nations of closing their doors to import products. Few agree on the causes, let alone the consequences of economic upheavals.

In each claim there is some measure of truth. But none of the assertions, singly or together, adequately explains the economic environment or how to compete within it.

What then *is* happening? There are three by no means exhaustive but definitely fundamental forces of change shaping the economic environment: (1) the growth of capital-intensive manufacturing; (2) the accelerated tempo of new technology; and (3) the concentrated pattern of consumption.

1

Finally, there is the jingoistic reaction to these forces—protectionism.

Together, these currents are reshaping patterns of power within industries, between industries, and across developed countries' economies, both among themselves and at the regional as well as the global level.

Let us briefly examine these interrelated forces from the standpoint of stress on existing industrial structures. We can then probe the strategic implications of these currents.

1

CAPITAL-INTENSIVE
OPERATIONS

CONSIDER, FIRST, the upheaval in production processes. Within the past decade automation, robots, machining centers, and numerical controls have increased productivity significantly in the broadest sense. These innovations have reduced the work force, expanded output per unit of time, allowed quick changeover from one type of manufacturing process to another, and permitted greater flexibility in plant siting. Translated into quantitative terms, the labor content of traditional assembly operations has dropped from 25 percent to somewhere between 10 and 5 percent of the total cost of the product.

In turn, the microchip's increased memory and intelligence has precipitated a steep decline in the cost of computer power. Together with automated production processes, computer-aided design and computer-aided manufacturing are begetting upheavals of their own.

The competitive repercussions of this shift from labor to capital in production are already evident in the automobile industry. The Japanese automobile industry, as a whole, produces over 13 million units a year and employs only 670,000 people. This includes the work force of all 11 automakers,

3

their component suppliers, and automobile contractors. In contrast, General Motors (GM) alone had a global work force of more than 690,000 persons at the end of 1983.

The cost of labor at Nissan is under 7 percent of total costs and it is less than 6 percent at Toyota. A direct comparison to U.S. labor costs is difficult because of the different ratio between components manufactured and purchased from other sources. But in fiscal 1981, when comparable data became available, the cost of labor for Ford (with an approximately 45 percent "make" ratio) was $10 billion; at General Motors (with a 70 percent "make" ratio), labor costs ran to $18 billion; at Toyota, the cost of labor was $1 billion. Even if Toyota's wage rates matched GM's dollar for dollar, Toyota's profit loss would be less than 1.1 percent from its recent 7 to 8 percent return on sales. The difference is not so much in the wage rate as in the labor content, that is, how many minutes does it take to produce a car?

Toyota, which produces 3.3 million units a year, has kept reducing production man-hours so as to maintain its employee level at about 45,000 persons during the past decade (prior to its merger with its sales company in 1983) while increasing its output 3.5 times. Nissan's productivity—which is about twice that of its global competitors—has taken the same route. These companies have changed the traditional labor-intensive auto industry into a capital-intensive industry.

The story is the same in electronics. During the past five years, the work force required to assemble a given consumer electronics product has been halved. Today, direct labor costs in this industry are, on average, down to 5 percent of total costs. Likewise, the semiconductor industry has become a fixed-cost, capital-intensive game, as opposed to the variable-cost, labor-intensive game of only half a decade ago.

The trend is even more prevalent in the continuous-processing industries—chemicals, textiles, steel, and so forth. In these industries automated control systems increase productivity and hence competitiveness. In two of Japan's leading steel mills, Nippon Steel and Nippon Kokan KK, the labor tab hovers around 10 percent of total costs.

4

Expense of Cheap Labor

Probably the most far-reaching implication of this shift from labor to capital is that it shatters the mirage of low-cost labor in developing countries. The rationale behind companies locating their operations in countries where low labor costs were available was to focus management attention on bringing down variable costs. True, labor costs in developing nations still are only one-third as high as in developed nations. However, now that the direct labor content in competitive companies represents less than 10 percent of total manufacturing costs, the advantage gained by using cheap labor is offset by the costs of transporting critical components to the production site from developed countries (as most developing countries do not have the requisite vendors and subcontractors), and the costs of insuring the finished products and transporting them to major markets.

It costs more to bring products from cheap labor countries to the major markets in the industrialized nations belonging to the Organization for Economic Cooperation and Development (OECD) than to produce them close to home. For example, the typical cost of transporting a color television set from Southeast Asia to the West Coast of the United States is 13 percent of free on board (FOB), including duties and insurance. As a result, savings in the labor cost up to 10 percent of the total cost are offset by the additional transportation cost. On top of this, if critical components have to be imported to these countries from Japan and Taiwan, which is usually the case, the net result of the trade-off would favor siting the production facility in the market area or in the area where important component parts are available. This move also makes sense in industries where new models are constantly superseding old ones and hence there are constant changes in molds, jigs and tools, and components. Consumer and office electronics has become largely a fashion industry, where "booms" are normally short-lived, and certainly a production location remote from the location of the core engineering group has become very inconvenient. As a result, the attractiveness of producing goods in developing countries (relative to OECD) has almost disappeared. The situation is often compounded by the shortage of a good labor force and the lack of qualified local managers in developing countries.

This cost factor is why most blue chip Japanese companies no longer seek out the cheaper labor offered initially by Korea, Taiwan, and Singapore, and subsequently by Thailand, Malaysia, Indonesia, and the Philippines. It is also the reason why some American and European semiconductor manufacturers who kept chasing cheaper labor in these countries have fallen behind in the integrated circuit/LSI market share. Many firms set up shop in low-wage countries only to discover that their total costs did not drop significantly, or did not stay low for very long. Nippon Electric Company has withdrawn production, particularly the labor-intensive packaging and bonding processes, from scattered sites in Southeast Asia and consolidated its operations in a highly automated plant in Kumamoto, Kyushu. Hitachi and Toshiba have followed Nippon Electric. The chip-makers have learned first-hand what CTV and textile industries discovered earlier: inexperienced labor must be trained and, once trained and experienced, labor does not stay cheap very long. Therefore, those who succumb to the mirage of cheap labor constantly migrate in pursuit of it. Right now, they are somewhere in India, Sri Lanka, or Indonesia. It is likely that they will all end up in the People's Republic of China where one billion people have just joined the low-wage labor market in Asia.

Flexibility of Options

Managers in automated industries who fail to recognize the implications of this shift from labor to capital will find their companies squeezed between spiraling inflation and excessive labor costs. The strategic ramifications of this fundamental shift include an increased ability of automated operations to fight inflation. The reason is that the ratio of labor costs to total manufacturing costs is bound to increase when compared to declining sales or inflated wages. Automated operations also resist recession. For example, highly automated facilities such as Yamazaki (machine tools) and Fujitsu Fanuc (numerical controls) are said to break even at 10 percent capacity; others like Toyota (passenger cars) claim that they can operate at 70 percent and still not lose money.

The other side of this shift from labor-intensive to capital-intensive industry is that it demands deep and immediate market penetration. This is vital to ensure the maximum economies of scale needed to defray heavy initial investment and to sustain the heavy outlays necessary for continued production process innovation. Domestic markets, even given the size of Japan or the United States, have proven to be too small for global-class automated plants in semiconductor and machine tools.

Therefore, it is more critical than ever before to be close to the market in order to keep product lines readily accepted by the majority of the target customers and in tune with competitive demands. New products that anticipate or serve user needs and the use of strongly entrenched distribution channels to reach prime markets may be key success factors, especially once a product reaches a "commodity" status and can be made by numerous competitors. At that stage, the opportunity to reduce costs to establish a competitive edge in a highly automated industry is pretty much the same for all participants. Since it has become very difficult to keep the product's competitiveness through differentiated technologies and design, it is mandatory that the company maintain the distribution capability to win the nondifferentiated game of "engineered commodities." Hence, these commodities are no different from sugar and cement, in which product differentiation is extremely difficult. Although it is very difficult to learn how to make a high-quality color television, as many as 30 companies around the world have mastered the art and can each now make products that are virtually indistinguishable in terms of quality. As a result, a company's ability to sell large volumes of nondifferentiated products at the lowest cost to the end user has become the key factor for survival.

THE ACCELERATING
TEMPO OF TECHNOLOGY

THE PRESENT UPHEAVAL in the production process is more than matched by the transformations in the industrial landscape wrought by state-of-the-art technologies. The interaction between scientific disciplines, between industries, and between industries and services is blurring the structural boundaries of existing economic power patterns. Further contributing to this structural upheaval is the accelerated pace of technological innovation and its commercialization. No longer does a superior technological edge guarantee success. No longer can most companies approach the marketplace by developing in their domestic market first.

To put this into proper perspective, consider the economic power of such vanguard industries as electronics, data processing, telecommunications, fine chemicals, and pharmaceuticals—to cite five of the more obvious high-technology industries. Together these industries, which constitute 6.1 percent of manufacturing gross national product (GNP) of the 24 OECD nations, accounted for 16 percent of these nations' economic growth from 1975 to 1980.

A recent comparison between high and medium technologies illustrates this economic power. The "highs" are the five cited above; the "mediums" are iron and steel, automobiles, organic chemistry, textiles, nonferrous metals, and pulp and paper industries. The comparison in OECD nations revealed that, on average, the high-technology group had 1.49 times the sales growth, 2.8 times the labor productivity growth, and 2.75 times the profit growth of the medium-technology industries. The high-technology group also is the one comprising the high value-added industries, as shown in Exhibit 2–1.

Exhibit 2–2 shows the net profit on sales of aggregate high-technology industries as contrasted to the aggregate of old-line industries. It has become very difficult to make money in old-line industries that have become "engineered commodities." Exhibit 2–3 shows the relative share of the Triad in terms of production and consumption. It shows that industries critical to wealth generation in the 1980s are all concentrated in Japan, the United States, and Europe: more than 80 percent of global production and consumption. Technological breakthroughs, in terms of patents registered as shown in Exhibit 2–4, are also taking place in Japan, the United States, and Europe.

The economic importance of vanguard industries is echoed from company to company, product line to product line. In a fast-paced consumer electronic goods firm, its line of videocassette recorders (VCRs) grew at three times the rate of its other audiovisual products. In a major chemical company, fine chemicals are generating two to four times the growth of bulk chemicals. The picture is, not surprisingly, the same in the distressed textile industry. Here, for example, the profit/sales ratio and the growth rate of Toray's newly developed carbon fiber products were twice that of its conventional synthetics.

If the profits are high, so, too, is the price tag. Toray, for example, reinvests 2.4 percent of its sales in research and development (R&D), an amount which is nearly three times that of the textile industry's average. The chemical company with high value-added fine chemical products spends nearly one-and-a-half times its industry average on R&D. And the consumer electronic firm that introduced a VCR ahead of

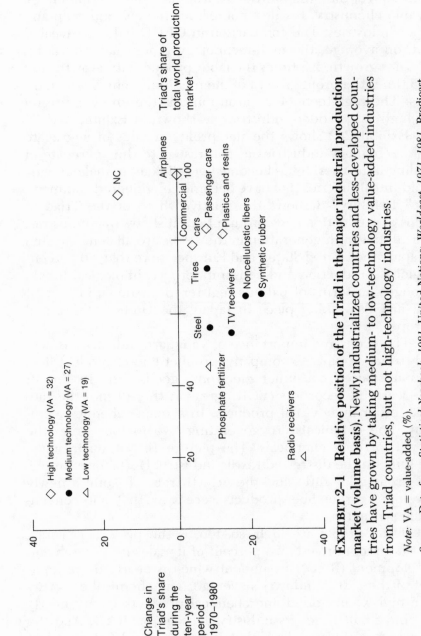

EXHIBIT 2–1   Relative position of the Triad in the major industrial production market (volume basis). Newly industrialized countries and less-developed countries have grown by taking medium- to low-technology value-added industries from Triad countries, but not high-technology industries.

Note: VA = value-added (%).

Source: Data from *Statistical Yearbook, 1981*, United Nations; *Worldcast, 1971, 1981*, Predicast, Cleveland, Ohio; McKinsey analysis.

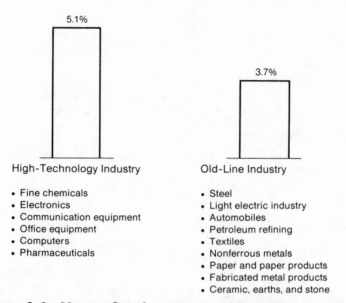

High-Technology Industry

- Fine chemicals
- Electronics
- Communication equipment
- Office equipment
- Computers
- Pharmaceuticals

Old-Line Industry

- Steel
- Light electric industry
- Automobiles
- Petroleum refining
- Textiles
- Nonferrous metals
- Paper and paper products
- Fabricated metal products
- Ceramic, earths, and stone

EXHIBIT 2–2   Net profit/sales ratio (world's leading companies: weighted average of 1980 and 1981). High-technology industries offer higher profitability opportunities.

Source: Data from *Economic Analysis of World Enterprise—International Comparison,* Japanese Ministry of International Trade and Industry, 1982.

its competitors recycles 7 percent of its sales (nearly double the industry norm) back into new product development.

Any corporation that lacks a firm position in the Triad will likely miss out on opportunities or face discontinuous risks. A major challenge for corporations in the remainder of the 1980s will be to revitalize activities throughout the Triad.

Intensified Integration and Cross-fertilization

As the development and commercialization of new technological breakthroughs become increasingly costly, there is a threefold movement toward integration and cross-fertilization: (1) downstream to control interfaces with the customer, (2) upstream to acquire new technologies and thereby cross the

11

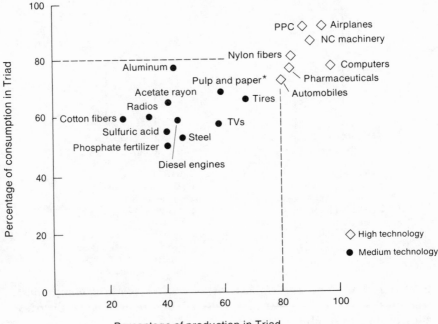

EXHIBIT 2–3 Share of the Triad in the world market: selected segments. Most high-tech products are still produced and consumed in the Triad.

Source: Data from McKinsey analysis of U.S. Department of Commerce *Statistical Abstract, 1981;* Nomura Research Institute; Japanese Ministry of Finance; *International Statistical Abstract,* The Prime Minister's Office of Japan, 1981.

"technological threshold" or to protect the supply of expensive raw materials, and (3) horizontally to share complementary technologies needed to create or exploit new market opportunities.

The first two moves are obvious. As global competition intensifies, management of fixed costs, particularly in R&D and distribution, becomes critical for creating wealth. The fixed cost of R&D, especially the cost of developing valuable breakthrough technologies, is becoming so high that, once developed, their global potential must be exploited to the fullest. This, however, requires that the corporations in posses-

12

By . . .

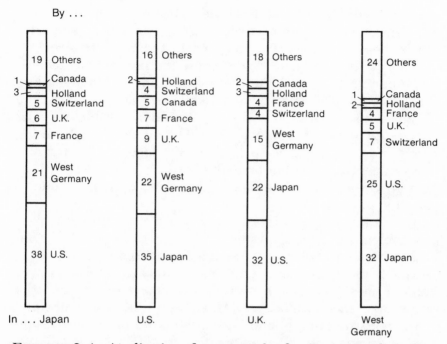

EXHIBIT 2–4 **Applications for patents by foreign nationals in Japan, the United States, the United Kingdom, and West Germany (1982; percent).** Most of the new technological developments occurred within the Triad.

Source: Data from *The Patent Agent Report,* The Patent Agency, Tokyo, Japan, 1984.

sion of such technologies have the ability to penetrate deeply into all critical markets. Most corporations, with the possible exception of IBM, Xerox, Kodak, and the like, do not have distribution networks capable of establishing an effective share of foreign markets comparable to their well-established domestic distribution channels. For example, Toyota and Nissan have a domestic market share of 38 percent and 28 percent, respectively, but their share is only 5 percent in the European Community[1] and 12 percent in the United States.[2] Even Sony has a mere 8 percent market share in the U.S. consumer television market,[3] while its share in Japan is 19 percent.[4]

A natural strategic move, therefore, is to concentrate on

13

strengthening R&D and domestic distribution. Once a corporation develops a unique technology, it can cross-license this technology to foreign counterparts in the other two regions of the Triad in order to (1) distribute the products to achieve high penetration, enabling the corporation to reduce marketing risks in difficult foreign markets, and at the same time (2) give the corporation, in return, attractive new technologies to be exploited in its home markets. This kind of cross-licensing increases a technology's potential by a factor of 2 to 3, and maximizes the contribution to the fixed cost of domestic distribution through the handling of foreign-originated products and technologies.

The third type of crossover is horizontal. In today's high-technology industries, no single company can control all critical technological elements, ranging from memory microchips, image sensors, and laser emitters to units to send data over phone lines, modems, optical transmission devices, and the time division multiplex (TDM) technique to send voice and data over the same phone line at the same time. As a result, any participant in office automation, robotics, and consumer electronics must develop a supersensitive control tower function to constantly scan and monitor externally available technologies and at the same time concentrate on fewer, critical internal R&D projects. In order to avoid discontinuous risks of losing out totally in a new game, a corporation may very well cross-fertilize with a complementary company, be it domestic or foreign, across a wide spectrum of the business system, that is, procurement, design, manufacturing, sales, customer engineering, and servicing.

The signposts of structural shifts on a cross-national basis are all there. Remember the technological patent exchange between the two leviathans in telecommunications and computers, respectively—Japan's Nippon Telegraph and Telephone (NTT) and America's IBM? There are others forging similar links in order to carve out a niche in an important emerging market, called telematics by the French and videotext by the Americans. Whatever it's called, the principle is the same: using telephone lines to link a given medium [word processor, personal computer, facsimile, cathode-ray tube (CRT), etc.] to allow individuals to do things like shop, bank, buy airline or theatre tickets, or receive and use other information.

The contenders vying for a piece of the potentially lucrative pie in computers and communication are coming from all directions. American Telephone and Telegraph (AT&T), for instance, not to be outdone by IBM's liaison with NTT, Matsushita, and Mitsubishi in Japan, is moving into IBM's computer turf in partnership with Philips and Olivetti in Europe. Although U.S. and Japanese participants have distinctly different origins, they appear destined to converge or merge before the final shakeout battle is won. Today's American contenders in the Japanese office automation (OA) equipment market include all the traditional and plug-in computer competitors, entrants from traditional "office equipment" makers (such as Xerox, Hewlett-Packard, and so forth), a host of word processor entrants led by Wang, and even a personal computer manufacturer or two.

Now, look at the 75 Japanese office automation leaders. This group includes general electric firms like Toshiba, Hitachi, and Mitsubishi Electric; home appliance companies like Matsushita, Sanyo, Sharp, and Sony; companies manufacturing cameras and plain paper copiers (PPCs), like Canon, Ricoh, Minolta, Konica (under Royal/U-Bix brands); companies applying component or microprocessor technology to other industries such as watches, musical instruments, and hand-held calculators; and process-control and measurement-instrument firms like Yokogawa and Omron, and sewing machine companies like Brother and Silver Reed.

Several of these contenders are arming themselves for the coming global battle for dominance through international alliances with competitors. Burroughs, which is trying to latch onto Hitachi's technological edge, is already packaging Fujitsu's high-speed facsimiles as part of its office automation offering and is manufacturing Nippon Electric Company's (NEC's) optical character reading techniques under a royalty license.

Toshiba's high-speed facsimiles are being distributed in

the United States by Pitney Bowes and Telautograph, a subsidiary of the Arden Group, and by International Telephone and Telegraph (ITT) in Europe.

Even now, as the divergent Japanese contenders and giant European computer and communications firms, each with different "core" strengths and economic bases, mingle with the more precisely defined American entrants in the office-automation fray, the entire structure of the industry is undergoing a major transition. Meanwhile, to build the volume needed to survive in what promises to be a hotly contested share war, most major global players are tapping their secondary markets. Japan is pushing its office automation products in Asia, while U.S. and European manufacturers both vie for a beachhead in Latin American markets. And everyone is hastening to establish a procurement agent in Eastern Asia to buy critical components and subassemblies such as keyboards, disk drives, CRTs, and printers.

Accelerated Diffusion of New Technology

The rapid rate of technological dispersal, although in large part a result of the interacting forces of change already mentioned, represents a distinct and important phenomenon of its own.

Consider these time frames. The first working computer was built in the 1920s. It took another 30 years to bring a digital computer from the development stage to a commercial product in 1954. The basic research on the transistor, which was developed at Bell Laboratories in 1947, was in progress for over a decade. The transistor was not commercially introduced, in hearing aids and telephone communications, until four years later. Another six years passed before it was incorporated into the computer.

The silicon microchip, first developed in 1956 by Texas Instruments (TI), then a small geophysics service firm, was superseded in three years by chemically produced chips. The integrated circuit, first developed in 1958 also by TI, took three years to become a viable product.

16

Now consider the accelerated time frame for major developments in the semiconductor during the past decade (Exhibit 2–5). It took two years in the United States for the chip to move from 4K-bit random access memory (RAM) to 16K. (Each K represents the capacity to hold about 1,000 units of information.) And it took less than eight months for the Japanese to catch up with the United States. It took two years for the United States to move from 16K to 32K chips and less than three months for Japan to catch up. Then, in 1977, Japan's NEC leapfrogged U.S. suppliers to introduce the 64K microchip. In 1983, the Japanese started sample shipment of the 256K N-MOS dynamic RAM, and early in 1984 they started its commercial production. American firms are lagging behind on average about one year.

The story is much the same in computers. The world dominance of IBM has been increasingly challenged by plug-in-compatible manufacturers that turn out computers that use IBM software as well as those of traditional rivals. In 1979, when IBM introduced its 4300 model, it took competitors five years to catch up. By 1983, when IBM introduced its powerful 308X model, it met competition head on.

While the incident involving Hitachi's and Mitsubishi's apparent theft of IBM's confidential software information will no doubt slow down their penetration into U.S. and European parts of the Triad, the technological lead of the U.S. mainframe makers has been narrowed. The rate of diffusion has become so fast that one can no longer assume a position of technological monopoly for long.

The strategic implications of this accelerated diffusion are threefold: first, technologically advanced companies cannot rest on their laurels for very long, if at all; second, the challengers with products that may only warrant an "A" instead of "AAA" or "prime" rating may still have the clout to erode the market share of the original product; third, since it costs dearly to develop a technologically advanced and differentiated product, the company must be able to sell simultaneously to the entire world in order to amortize the heavy front-end investment. The bottom line is that companies that choose to develop domestic markets first before moving on to over-

17

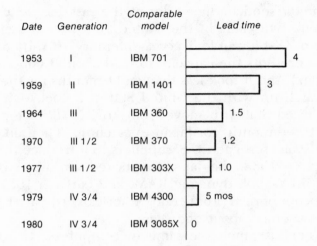

Computer

Date	Generation	Comparable model	Lead time
1953	I	IBM 701	4
1959	II	IBM 1401	3
1964	III	IBM 360	1.5
1970	III 1/2	IBM 370	1.2
1977	III 1/2	IBM 303X	1.0
1979	IV 3/4	IBM 4300	5 mos
1980	IV 3/4	IBM 3085X	0

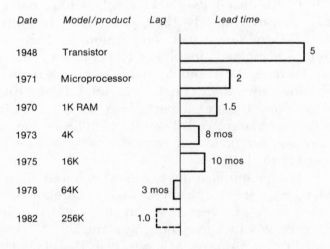

Integrated Circuit

Date	Model/product	Lag	Lead time
1948	Transistor		5
1971	Microprocessor		2
1970	1K RAM		1.5
1973	4K		8 mos
1975	16K		10 mos
1978	64K	3 mos	
1982	256K	1.0	

* Time between U.S. development and Japanese catch-up.

EXHIBIT 2–5 Technological lead time* of the United States over Japan (years). The technological lead time between countries has almost disappeared.

Source: Data from Hitachi and Matsushita (Yasuo Okamoto); *Computopia* (April 1981); *Management* (October 1979).

seas markets may find themselves totally blocked out by competitors that are well entrenched and ready to launch an offensive on others' home markets.

The history of the VCR market is a good example (Exhibit 2–6). Here's what happened. Soon after the VCR's introduc-

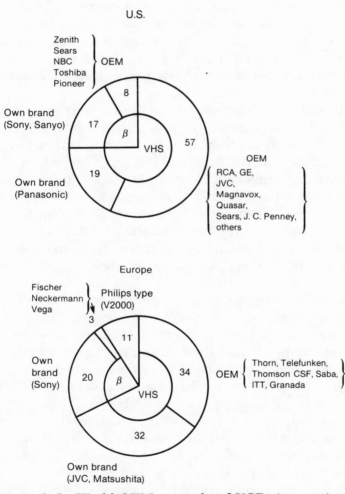

EXHIBIT 2–6 World OEM networks of VCRs (percent).

Source: TV Digest, quoted by *Los Angeles Times,* January 18, 1984; *The Wall Street Journal,* Eastern SP edition, February 4, 1984; *Financial Times,* April 1, 1984; *Les Echos,* March 26, 1982.

tion, Sony and the Matsushita group [Victor Company of Japan (JVC), Panasonic, Technics, and Quasar] each developed a different type of competitive product [Beta and video home system (VHS), respectively] and moved—both directly and through consortia alliances—to capture markets in all three parts of the Triad simultaneously. Sony franchised Toshiba and Sanyo and allied with Zenith and Sears in the United States, and now has 35 percent of that market. In Europe, Sony used Fischer in the United Kingdom, Neckermann in Germany, and Vega in Spain. But Sony fared better with its own distribution channels. It now has captured 23 percent of the European Community market.

Matsushita's success was even more startling. In the United States, it captured a 15 percent share through its own outlets, but gained another 45 percent as an original equipment manufacturer (OEM) supplier to RCA, Magnavox, General Electric, Sylvania, and Montgomery Ward, among others. In Europe, Matsushita's affiliated company, JVC, swallowed up an impressive 68 percent of the market: 33 percent through its own channels, and the remainder as an OEM supplier to EMI and Thorn in the United Kingdom, Telefunken in Germany, Thomson CSF in France, Saba in Norway, and Granada in Spain.

Toshiba and Hitachi, despite technology and distribution channels at home, just didn't move fast enough, and remain at a low percentage share in overseas markets. Some companies have had to change their strategy. Philips announced, in late 1983, plans to produce VHS models in Europe[5] in addition to its own V2000, and Toshiba announced, in October 1984, an offering of both Beta and VHS in Japan, a major setback for Sony in an industry where compatibility is so crucial. These examples illustrate how critical it has become to preempt opportunities of other major contenders in the Triad when there is a compatibility issue, such as Beta versus VHS.

Another lesson is that speed has become a critical element of global strategy. All important markets must be penetrated simultaneously. That's why consortia alliances with strong regional corporations are frequently better choices than the

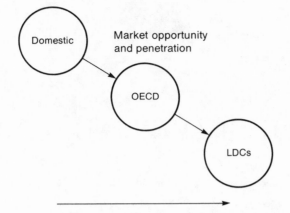

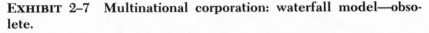

EXHIBIT 2–7 **Multinational corporation: waterfall model—obsolete.**

slow-but-steady, do-it-alone approach. The waterfall model (Exhibit 2–7), which has been used implicitly by many traditional multinational corporations (MNCs), has become obsolete. The assumption that the home country's strengths and success can be transferred to other OECD nations, and eventually to less-developed countries (LDCs), can betray a company, particularly in fast-moving high-technology industries.

THE UNIVERSAL USERS

CAPITAL GOODS USERS have become fairly concentrated. As a case in point, take the structure of the electronics industry worldwide.

According to statistics amassed by the OECD, in 1970 the total demand for computers was $56.8 billion, in 1975 demand for computers hit $91.3 billion, and by 1985 demand is projected to reach $204.8 billion—reflecting a growth rate nearly double that of most national economies. The production share distributed to five major countries (the United States, Japan, West Germany, the United Kingdom, and France) was on the order of 85 percent. In the case of numerically controlled machine tools, 70 percent were distributed to Japan, United States, and West Germany alone.

This concentration in capital electronic goods was more than matched by consumer electronic goods. Again, the same five nations within the Triad accounted for 82 percent of the demand for electronic consumer goods in 1975.

What these statistics point to is that a company that ignores the universal market potential of the Triad does so at its own peril. For example, not too long ago manufacturers of capital equipment produced machinery that reflected strong cultural distinctions. West German machines reflected that nation's penchant for craftsmanship; American equipment was often extravagant in its use of raw materials. But these distinctions have disappeared. The best-selling factory machines have lost the "art" element which distinguished them and have become both in appearance and in the level of skills they require much more similar. The current revolution in production engineering has brought ever-increasing global standards of performance. In an era when productivity improvements can quickly determine their life or death on a global scale, companies cannot afford to indulge themselves in a metallic piece of art that will last 30 years.

At the same time, consumer products customers have become fairly homogeneous. The Triad consumption pattern, which is both a cause and an effect of cultural patterns, has its roots to a large extent in the educational system. As educational systems enable more people to use technology, they tend to become more similar to each other. It follows, therefore, that education leading to higher levels of technological achievement also tends to eradicate differences in life-styles. Penetration of television, which enables everyone possessing a television set to share sophisticated behavioral information instantaneously throughout the world, has also accelerated this trend. There are, for example, 600 million consumers in all three parts of the Triad (Japan, the United States, the nations of the European Community) with strikingly similar needs and preferences. Gucci bags, Sony Walkmans, and McDonald's hamburger stands are seen on the streets of Tokyo, London, Paris, and New York. A new generation worships the universal "now" gods—"ABBA, Levi's, and Arpege."

In other words, within the Triad countries, the generation gap—the vertical difference between age groups—is more pronounced than the difference of tastes across the national boundaries. Youngsters in Denmark, West Germany, Japan, and California are all growing up with ketchup, jeans, and guitars. Their life-styles, aspirations, and desires are so similar that you might call them "OECDites" or Triadians, rather than by names denoting their national identity. The younger generation of Triadians may be called "The New Californians," or "The Angels" after their capital, Los Angeles. Except for the language and hair color, you can't tell the nationality of a youngster in Tokyo's Harajuku who walks around in Nike sneakers, L.L. Bean shorts, and an Izod sportshirt, carrying a Prince tennis racket (for the fun of it) and a Louis Vuitton bag. Seen as a consumer, this youngster's nationality is far less important than his or her basic wants and aspirations. Likewise, a typical New York businessman might be hardly distinguishable from his counterparts in Tokyo or Dusseldorf—each wears a dark-blue suit, Regal shoes, and a Celine necktie, carries a Casio pocket calculator in his Mark Cross wallet, frequents a nearby *sushi* bar for lunch, and commutes in a Celica.

What are the reasons for the similarities and commonalities in the Triad's consumer demand and life-style patterns? The first is purchasing power. The purchasing power of Triad residents, as expressed in discretionary income per individual, is more than ten times greater than that of residents of less-developed countries and newly industrialized countries (NICs) (Exhibit 3–1). Penetration of television into households in Triad countries is greater than 94 percent,[1] whereas that for NICs is about 60 percent,[2] and that for LDCs is less than 10 percent.[3] One-third of the Japanese–U.S. consumers graduate from senior high school or higher educational institutions,[4] but a comparable level of education still is offered to less than 15 percent of the population in NICs,[5] and to an even lower percentage in LDCs. It is their education level, what they read and see, and their purchasing power that really makes the Triadians behave similarly to each other and that distinguishes them from the rest of the world.

Another set of forces at work which is pushing the Triadians in the same direction with respect to the demand pattern is the similarities in their technological infrastructure. For example, over 50 percent of Triadian households have a telephone. This in turn creates a hospitable environment for products like facsimile, telex, and digital data transmission/processing equipment.

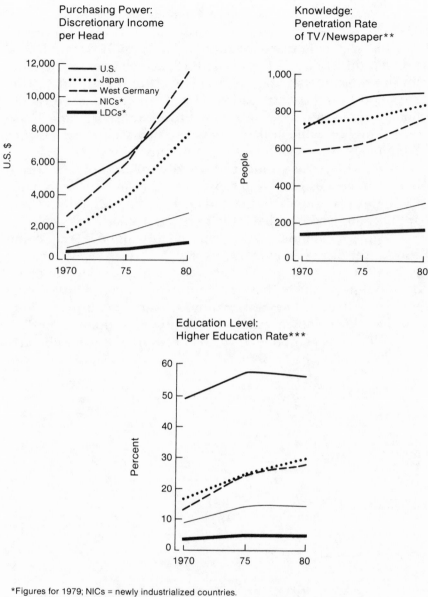

Purchasing Power:
Discretionary Income
per Head

Knowledge:
Penetration Rate
of TV/Newspaper**

Education Level:
Higher Education Rate***

*Figures for 1979; NICs = newly industrialized countries.

**Penetration rate of media = TV receivers per 1,000 people + newspaper circulation per 1,000 people.

***Higher education rate = $\dfrac{\text{No. of students in university and equivalent institutions}}{\text{Population of 20–24 year old people (Japan = 18–22 years old)}}$

EXHIBIT 3–1 Universal users have emerged within the Triad as a result of greater commonality among these countries.

Source: Data from *Statistical Yearbook, 1979, 1981* (United Nations); *International Statistical Yearbook, 1981, 1983,* The Prime Minister's Office of Japan; *Statistical Yearbook, 1983,* UNESCO.

In Triad countries, the number of physicians[6] per 10,000 population as of 1979 exceeded 18, which creates demand for pharmaceuticals and medical electronics. The higher ratio of paved to nonpaved roads in Triad countries is the reason for the rapid penetration of radial tires and sportscars. These are all higher value-added products. They also require higher technology to produce and/or to design them.

Once these commonalities are recognized, universal products can be designed. This pattern of brand usage is new. Conceptually, this is illustrated in Exhibit 3–2. While there are certain products that have to be tailor-made to each market segment, the increasing commonality among Triad countries in terms of life-style means that a company has a greater chance of winning in the race for consumer acceptance by developing products that will be universally used on a global basis. Companies like Seiko, Sony, Canon, Matsushita, Casio, and Honda are now routinely developing products according to a "global" perspective. Instead of communicating indirectly

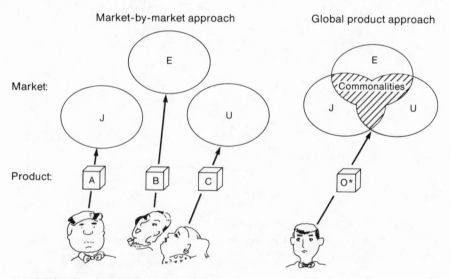

Market-by-market approach   Global product approach

*600 million OECD-ites in Triad.

EXHIBIT 3–2 Strategies should be developed to capitalize on similarities and potential for shared resources.

26

with users and distributors, product designers of these companies personally spend as much as half of their time abroad directly talking with their customers and dealers. When they return, another half of their time is spent in designing and synthesizing the global product directly out of their personal impressions.

This concentration of consumer and capital goods users within Europe, Japan, and the United States is probably the primary Triad trigger for high-technology competition. The Triad is where the main action is. Corporations still wrapped up in the "United Nations" approach, seeking a market presence in each of the 150 countries of the world, often find their resources suddenly depleted. Or, such a company ends up having problems competing with other firms, and encounters problems making a profit in a larger and highly competitive market, for example, the Triad countries, but does very well in small and strategically unimportant countries. Over time, the performance of a firm becomes inversely proportional to the significance of each market it enters.

NEOPROTECTIONISM

PROTECTIONISM IS BOTH a cause and an effect of fundamental change crumbling established economic pillars. Any attempt to gauge what triggered the last recession—uncompetitive labor costs, failure to invest, high cost of capital, seesawing exchange rates, trade imbalance—is somewhat like trying to determine which came first, the chicken or the egg.

In the end, one fact remains unchanged. Most Free World economies were in a severe slump in the early 1980s, and they all bounced back as the U.S. Presidential election approached in 1984. High unemployment has contributed to decreased purchasing power which, in turn, has led to slowdowns in the automobile, consumer goods, and construction industries and dependent businesses, such as steel and component parts. New technologies are adding to the economic dislocation. Automation, as we have noted, requires changes in the labor force and, when workers are not retrained, we are confronted with the paradoxical situation of high unemployment and a shortage of special skills which cannot be automated.

The resulting economic condition makes it very difficult for national leaders and politicians to resist short-term remedies. Trade barriers are one response. There are, however, two grave dangers inherent in protectionism. One is a chain reaction at the national level. Measures to support one group give legitimacy to claims from others, and products from "protected" industries lessen the competitiveness of those who use them in producing still other goods. A "protected" steel industry will weaken the auto industry since the latter must consume the former's product. The second danger is that protectionism carries the seeds of international reaction.

Then, too, there's the matter of economic power. Protectionist measures, which frequently evade established international rules, concentrate power among a few politicians and bureaucrats.

It is not our intent here to exhaust the causes of this obvious current, but rather to acknowledge its reality and to alert corporations to its implications. To state the obvious: if you are not an "insider" in a country important to your share growth, you just may find the doors to its markets tightly closed.

Exhibit 4-1 is a summary of regulations by country. Some countries set up quotas and high duties against all imports, and others against imports coming from Japan or other specific countries. At any rate, the net impact of these regulations is that unless you become a recognized insider, your trade base is always fragile. During the uproar against Japanese color television in the United States, Sony, because it has a sizable plant in San Diego, was not lumped together with other Japanese color television producers and was insulated from the quotas and surcharges.

One important message for pragmatic businesspeople to remember is that these governmental regulations and journalistic outcries do not necessarily reflect the voice of the public at large. For example, because the Japanese government enters into a tough negotiation with the United States Trade Representative (USTR) on orange and beef quotas does not mean the Japanese people are against buying U.S. oranges and beef. In fact, they welcome high-quality, low-price food from any country. Likewise, we do have to recognize that

Regulations by Country

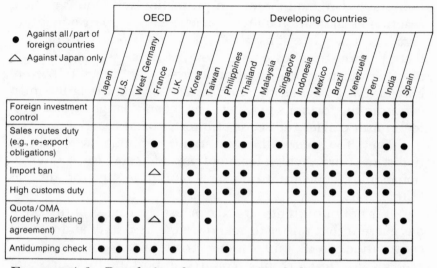

Legend:
● Against all/part of foreign countries
△ Against Japan only

	OECD					Developing Countries												
	Japan	U.S.	West Germany	France	U.K.	Korea	Taiwan	Philippines	Thailand	Malaysia	Singapore	Indonesia	Mexico	Brazil	Venezuela	Peru	India	Spain
Foreign investment control						●	●	●	●	●		●	●		●	●	●	●
Sales routes duty (e.g., re-export obligations)			●			●		●	●		●		●				●	●
Import ban				△		●		●	●			●	●	●	●	●	●	
High customs duty						●	●	●	●			●	●	●	●	●	●	
Quota/OMA (orderly marketing agreement)	●	●	●	△	●	●											●	●
Antidumping check	●	●	●	●	●			●						●			●	●

EXHIBIT 4–1 **Regulations by country.** Trade barriers and foreign capital restrictions increase corporations' need to become "insiders."

Source: Overseas Market Series, Japan External Trade Organization (JETRO); *International Trade & Foreign Exchange Systems, 1983—IMF Annual Report,* JETRO; *Trade Yearbook, 1984,* Japan Tariff Association; *The Customs Tariff of the World,* Japan Tariff Association, March 1984; *Trade & Customs,* Japan Tariff Association, February 10 and March 10, 1984.

the American people like to buy Japanese color televisions and automobiles. People at large want the best product for the price from anywhere in the world.

That is the reason for increasing transnational trade, and hence trade friction. The governmental and social forces, however, oftentimes act counter to these basic forces, and create artificial hurdles to the transnational flow of goods. My assertion is that you have to establish a de facto insider position which is relatively uninfluenced by the unexpected and/or abrupt man-made barriers.

It is a sad fact that the fragmentation of the developed markets is taking place (and seemingly even intensifying) at a time when the residents of the Triad are emerging almost as a homogeneous buying group. Pragmatic business strategists, therefore, must address these two opposite phenomena simultaneously by developing the Triad perspective and yet also by accelerating a company's "insiderization" in key markets.

Against these four major currents that are reshaping the global enterprise, I believe we need to recap Part I and reexamine the viability of the existing models for a multinational corporation:

1. *Clee's model* is no longer adequate as we cannot really profitably locate the production plant in low-labor-cost countries. As robots and automated machines have reduced the labor factor, the benefits of lower wages are disappearing rapidly. Robots and computer-aided design/computer-aided manufacturing (CAD/CAM), unlike the automation machines in the 1960s and the 1970s, have increased flexibility in coping with rapid model changes and handling multiple product lines coming on a single conveyor belt.

Coupled with the neoprotectionist pressures, production sites need to be located where an abundant (value-adding) engineering force is available at the customer interface and where the production plant can be labeled an insider (as opposed to an invader) in the Triad's major markets.

2. *The United Nations model* leads to running into the jungles and unattractive markets. If its headquarters is located at a psychological equidistance to all of the 150 countries in the world, together with their widely different infrastructures and economic environments, a corporation is likely to run into several problems and/or discontinuities in countries that are unimportant in the marketplace.

In order to reverse the situation, a corporation has to send in a fairly competent group of managers to a rather insignificant market. Even if the situation in small markets is reversed, the net positive impact would be negligible compared with the insignificant positions the corporation it has managed to establish in the key countries of the Triad. In fact, a strong presence in small markets is hardly a guarantee protecting the company against eventual invasion by the Triad's strong competitors, nor is a strong position in small

31

markets important enough to offset a company's miserable situation in the key markets. The United Nations model invites uneven distribution of management resources against the potential market size and/or strategic needs of establishing a viable position there. During the 1970s, many European multinationals concentrated their efforts in Latin America, Africa, and the Middle East, only to find themselves far behind the Americans and the Japanese in the high-technology race in the key Triad markets.

3. *The waterfall model* is outdated today, as technological diffusion happens so fast that no one can stay in the lead for long. "Being first" is no guarantee for "being the best" or "being the biggest" in today's world, when a company is in business competition with the world's toughest and nimblest firms.

The competitive power of any corporation no longer means monopolization. The key factor for success of a business in most industries has shifted downstream, toward the customer end of the business system, which is the most difficult element to change in a hurry. Upstream functions, such as purchasing and manufacturing, cannot be differentiated, as most of these functions have become commodities; the products also have become "engineered commodities" with hardly any differentiation. The source of this differentiation really lies in image, logistics, distribution, service, and degree of perfection in execution. The outdated waterfall model assumes a sequential conquering of key markets over a rather prolonged period of time. What is needed today is a "sprinkler" model which, using the hyperpressure from the roof, floods the key markets simultaneously within a few seconds after the opening of the valve.

One of the means to accomplish this is the formation of a Triad consortium. However, before we talk about how a company goes about establishing itself as a Triad power, we need to take a detour to examine the changing nature of global competition, and the net result of recognizing and not recognizing such changes.

PART II

THE REALITIES OF GLOBAL COMPETITION

AT MCKINSEY we use a framework called the business system. It is useful to discuss alternative approaches to global business, so let me take a moment to explain it. The business system is a description of functions necessary to operate a business. The business system of a fully integrated manufacturing company consists of technology, product design, manufacturing, marketing, sales, distribution and service functions (Exhibit II–1). The "upstream" functions of the business system appear on the left side of Exhibit II–1 and the "downstream" functions on the right side. Not all businesses entail all functions. For example, the business system of a distributor is limited to purchasing, sales, and service functions.

The business system concept can be used to emphasize or deemphasize functions. For example, we can add customer financing between marketing and sales to emphasize the importance of the financing function. We can deemphasize certain headquarters staff functions, such as personnel and accounting, by omitting them from the business system. This omission is not unusual because these functions, while serving to secure resources or lubricate corporate activities, are not directly responsible for carrying out the business in question.

Key Issues

Technology	Product design	Manufacturing	Marketing	Distribution	Sales
• Source	• Function	• Integration	• Prices	• Channels	• Warranty
• Sophistication	• Physical	• Technology	• Advertising/	• Integration	• Speed
• Patents	characteristics	• Raw materials	promotion	• Inventory	• Captive/
• Product/	• Aesthetics	• Capacity	• Sales force	• Warehousing	independent
process	• Quality	• Location	• Package	• Transport	• Prices
choices		• Procurement	• Brand		

EXHIBIT II–1   The business system.

The business system can also be used to describe a corporation's strategic actions:

△ A joint venture of manufacturing concerns can be described as two companies sharing manufacturing functions.

△ A technical licensing agreement can be described as the purchase of a technology.

△ Manufacturing in a developing country can mean splitting the business system between two countries.

△ Direct production in a foreign country requires transferring the whole business system, not just the marketing and sales functions. Japanese manufacturers often find direct production in the United States or European Community difficult because the purchasing, engineering, and manufacturing infrastructure there is very different from that in Japan.

△ Transnational mergers are effected to merge individual functions of the two companies across the national boundary so as to achieve economies of scale. But some European transnational mergers have been incompatible and unproductive because business system functions were not truly merged. Rather, the individual companies remained basically independent—and at times even competitive, and each function was left untouched, sacrificing the intended economies of scale.

Now let us use the idea of a business system to illustrate corporate strategies that support global activities.

GLOBAL IMPASSE

WE ARE SO ACCUSTOMED to the words "international competition" and "trade war" that it has become common to fear overseas competitors. That fear was certainly justified for two companies, Kaijirushi and Feather, which were once dominant in the Japanese razor market. They lost in their home market to Schick and Gillette, whose combined share of the Japanese wet shaving "changeable blade" razor market is now 80 percent.[1] Thousands of cottage bottling industries, including the Saida and Ramne cider drinks, were wiped out by Coca-Cola. Likewise, four Japanese motorcycle manufacturers—Honda, Yamaha, Kawasaki, and Suzuki—have triumphed over their worldwide competitors. These four had been the survivors of a fierce domestic race in addition, because in Japan in the 1950s there had been over 200 motorcycle manufacturers.

However, these kinds of dominant winners on the global scale are too few and too far between to allow generalizations. Today we are witnessing just the opposite to those success stories:

35

△ Even the most powerful and dominant companies at home are having difficulty repeating their performance abroad, especially in the key Triad markets of Japan, the United States, and Europe—a phenomenon of global impasse.

△ A company is more likely to be wiped out by strong domestic competitor(s) than by a foreign invader.

Let us look at several key markets to understand the nature of global competition.

Passenger Cars

In the case of automobiles, nine Japanese manufacturers have a cost advantage of close to a factor of 2 in 1,000- to 2,000-cc-class passenger cars over their U.S. and European competitors. However, even taking into account their "phenomenal" penetration into the OECD market, the highest penetration achieved by any of the nine companies has been Nissan's 6 percent in the United Kingdom,[2] only one fifth of its share at home.[3] Toyota's biggest success is in the United States, where it has 6 percent of the market.[4] That's far less than the share Volkswagen once enjoyed during its golden "beetle" days of the late 1960s, and now it's only one fifth of Toyota's presence at home.[5]

Even Honda, whose performance overseas is much more impressive than at home, has not done as well abroad. Honda, originally in the motorbike segment until the energy crisis, made a timely entry into the four-wheel segment with its fuel-efficient and clean CVCC engine in the early 1970s. Honda's motorcycles established a dominant share in overseas markets, exceeding 34 percent.[6] However, despite its international expertise and 74 percent export ratio,[7] the highest penetration of its passenger cars has been 4 percent in the United States,[8] or one third of its share at home.[9]

Early 1981 was a critical time for Japanese automakers;

their U.S. sales exceeded 20 percent of total U.S. car sales.[10] Thus, responding to the pressure created by the overall Japanese automobile presence in the United States, the Japanese agreed to a voluntary quota of 1.68 million units a year for 1982 and 1983. This number corresponds to approximately 17 percent of the total U.S. market for the nine Japanese passenger car companies (Toyota, Nissan, Honda, Toyo Kogyo–Mazda, Mitsubishi, Fuji Heavy Industries–Subaru, Isuzu, Suzuki, and Daihatsu). Each company's share was allocated on the basis of their prequota 1981 sales, so the top three manufacturers had the largest allocation. Agreeing to this quota meant that the nine companies had to give up the prospect of dominating the U.S. market or even coming close to Chrysler's U.S. share of around 9 percent.[11]

In mid-1983, the U.S. Trade Representative recommended extending the quota into 1984. Some U.S. companies, notably General Motors, which has an equity position in Isuzu and Suzuki, is reported to have favored the removal of the quota in order to import cars produced by their Japanese affiliates. More interesting was the position of the top three Japanese auto companies, Toyota, Nissan, and Honda. Not surprisingly, they publicly urged removing the quota, noting that in 1981 the United States requested the quota as a temporary measure to help the U.S. auto industry recover.

However, their private position was quite different. During this period Toyota, Nissan, and Honda enjoyed very high profits because of the extremely attractive U.S. price levels. In addition, these profits were virtually guaranteed because the quota allocation reduced the possibility of competition from the smaller Japanese auto companies for market share. Lifting the quota would restore free competition and likely reduce price levels and thus profits. Of course, the six less-favored companies were very eager to have the quota lifted so that they could further penetrate the United States market.

The result is that the United States and Japan agreed to extend the voluntary quota and raise it slightly, to 1.86 million units into 1984. This situation is quite acceptable to the Japanese Top Three—Toyota, Nissan, and Honda: the United

States is too important a market to risk being disturbed by lesser compatriots who, under different circumstances, might make all-out efforts to carve out bigger pieces of the pie for themselves.

The United States is not alone in employing trade restrictions to protect its automobile industry. In the auto-producing countries of each Triad area, the share of market claimed by the indigenous manufacturers has stabilized: 43 percent in the United Kingdom, 72 percent in the United States, 73 percent in West Germany, 67 percent in France, 63 percent in Italy, and 99 percent in Japan.[12] In other words, after a period of about 10 years, these nations have found that the way to "compete" with foreign invaders is, most often, to keep them out.

Medical Electronics

It has been some time since the medical electronics (ME) industry first became a lucrative "high-technology" sensation. And continued intense international competition for *the* leading position in the global market has made this industry a standard business school example.

And yet, despite the heated competition, it seems that yesterday's winners of the X-ray machine market have managed to maintain, and even enhance, their domestic position. The winners are Philips of Holland, Siemens of West Germany, General Electric of the United States, and Toshiba of Japan. These four companies fight head-on in each country for market share in almost all product areas.

Despite their efforts, however, none of them has "beaten" the others on their competitors' home turf. For example, the ME industry experienced a shock in the form of the CT scanner (X-ray computer tomography) developed by the innovative British firm, EMI. It didn't take long for the Big Four (Philips, Siemens, General Electric, Toshiba) to master the CT scanner and gain a share of the CT market in much the same way as they gained a share of the X-ray photographic equipment market. EMI, after a fairly strong start, had difficulty in continuing product innovation and penetrating major markets. Its technological inventiveness gave it only a few years of lead time, too short a period to establish its name and a full business system in the conservative practice of medicine.

Likewise, in the mid-1970s, Toshiba developed a CT scanner that uses ultrasonic waves. Sonic CT was revolutionary because, unlike the X-ray, which is not very effective in mapping soft tissue like the stomach and intestines, the sonic CT can clearly "see" and examine these organs. Counting on the strength of its sonic CT, Toshiba tried to penetrate the key markets in the Triad. To date, however, it has been unable to establish more than a few percentage point share in the world's major markets.

In both cases, technology was diffused more quickly than the establishment of distribution and service networks. Here is the dilemma: building market share overseas requires an effective distribution network and unique, differentiated, and strong products; however, setting up the distribution network entails high fixed costs and high risks. If a distribution network is developed first in anticipation of a "superproduct," a large amount of front-end money must be spent, which might not be recovered should the product not arrive on time or in first-rate shape. Keeping distributors interested in your product would also demand a certain level of investment every year, in terms of incentives and a national media campaign to support them.

Conversely, if a superproduct is developed and well accepted by the users at home, the news of the product quickly spreads, and competitors in major markets speedily develop a comparable model. When the creator of the product arrives in the countries where these markets exist, this firm finds that customers have already been captured or franchised by domestic establishments.

Medical electronics is not a high-technology industry, that is, it is not technology-driven. Rather, the customer end of the business system is of greatest importance. The relationship with medical doctors (the users and often the decision-makers for purchasing new equipment) is the key factor for success. "Maintaining the relationship" is a rather dull fixed-cost game. A fixed-cost game is also a painful game for a small firm. If the ante for playing the game is elevated to $100, it would wipe out any small citizens who happen to be trying out their luck for the evening.

Keeping close to the customer is called "relationship management." In the medical field, that means everything from clipping interesting medical articles from journals for the customer, to developing slides for a doctor's academic presentation, not to mention playing golf with the customer on weekends. In Japan, that's the role of the salesperson. In some cases, maintaining the relationship means repairing the sophisticated equipment overnight. It also means being prepared to respond to customers' unexpected demands. For example, a small cardiograph company provides an interesting service to its customers. Salespeople will pick up cardiograms from their customers, the doctors, and deliver them to a nearby expert doctor for diagnosis. This small company, unable to offer other amenities, apparently promised the service to doctors who would buy their equipment.

It is extremely difficult to challenge a time-honored, trust-based relationship. While not all Japanese doctors demand servantlike salespeople, in general their demands must be met before equipment can be sold. Foreign companies have difficulty accepting, let alone meeting, the sometimes excessive demands of Japanese doctors. Toshiba employs about 1,000 highly educated and flexible salespeople to do that[13]—and they do it quite well. Other equally technologically competent companies, such as Hitachi and Shimadzu, have been unable to shake Toshiba's dominant share position at 21 percent of the overall Japanese ME market.[14]

A relationship-based network, once established, is usually stable and can accommodate technological and other types of changes. That is why the Big Four have survived technological discontinuities and seem to be well positioned to cope with even tougher technological breakthroughs, such as the digital radiography that replaced X-ray film, and the NMR (nuclear magnetic resonance) scanner, which measures abnormal patterns of NMR in, for example, cancerous tissues.

In sum, the ME industry, and other industries whose customer end of the business system is crucial, find that even the most technologically advanced corporations have difficulty in capturing a stable share position in key overseas markets.

Consumer Electronics

In the early 1970s, trade friction over Japanese color television peaked. Following the oil shock, most Japanese color television companies shifted to integrated circuit technology, reduced the number of components by half, and automated production plants. These steps enabled them to produce a high-quality color television at less than half the price of U.S. and European manufacturers. Shocked by this danger to their markets, most countries hurried to set a quota and/or raise customs duties on Japanese color televisions to protect domestic color television manufacturers.

Japanese companies countered by stepping up domestic production and/or setting up direct production plants in the United States and Europe, for example, Sony in San Diego and Dorson (U.K.), Panasonic in Chicago (by acquiring Motorola's Quasar) and Cardiff (Wales), Sanyo in Arkansas, and Toshiba in Tennessee. These companies invested huge sums of money and, more importantly, management time, to further penetrate the key markets.

Results, today, indicate that Western tactics have succeeded. None of the companies mentioned above have substantially increased their share of the market in the key Triad countries. Sony, which has a 19 percent share of the Japanese market,[15] has only an 8 percent share in the United States[16] and around 5 percent in the European Community.[17] Matsushita, with its mighty sales force and 44,000 franchised outlets in Japan,[18] enjoys, on average, 30 percent home market share,[19] and less than 10 percent (Panasonic and Quasar com-

41

bined) in the United States and 5 percent in the European Community.[20] In addition, it seems that Japanese companies' combined share of market in each region has not grown beyond around 20 percent.[21] In the United States, Zenith and RCA still lead the market with a 20 percent share apiece.[22] This picture is dramatically different from the generally accepted success story of Japanese color television manufacturers.

Today, the color television industry is structurally troubled. Unlike the 1970s, when Western manufacturers were faced with a profit squeeze from the competitive and dynamic Japanese manufacturers, today hardly any company—including the Japanese—is making money producing color televisions except for once-in-four-years, that is, in every Presidential election year. Although a color television is a sophisticated piece of equipment, it has become an "engineered commodity." Everyone producing a color television has the same costs and a comparable technological level, using critical components and subassemblies purchasable from leading global parts suppliers.

As evidenced by the recent takeover of Grundig—first attempted unsuccessfully by France's Thomson CSF and finally successfully by Holland's Philips—true competitors who can have a rapid and strong impact on an industry tend to be domestic or regional. From within the Triad region, they are not necessarily foreign companies. Very few Japanese companies would have had the guts to take over a giant like Grundig: they don't know how to run such an established company; rather, they would prefer to start on the "green field" from a grass roots level. In the United States, the gains from Japanese takeovers of color television companies have been much smaller than expected. These advances amount to only a 5 percent gain for Matsushita in Motorola/Quasar, and a 5 percent gain for Sanyo in the Warwick takeover.

This unimpressive showing has not gone unnoticed by other companies. Therefore, it is very unlikely that companies like Hitachi, Mitsubishi, and Sharp will be interested in taking over other U.S. or European color television manufacturers.

42

Thus, we can draw two conclusions in the color television industry and, for that matter, in the mainstream consumer electronics industries: (1) the status quo established thus far is likely to remain for a long time, and (2) if there is any major change in the balance of power, it will, in all likelihood, be caused by compatriots. This would mean that the battle is, for example, between Sony and Matsushita in Japan, Zenith and RCA or General Electric in the United States, and Thorn-EMI and Philips in the United Kingdom.* [23]

Film

Globally, virtually only four film manufacturers have survived: Kodak, Fuji, Agfa, and Sakura. While Kodak dominates in most countries, in Japan it takes a backseat to Fuji, which has nearly 70 percent share of the market. Agfa has a strong position in Europe, especially in Germany and Belgium, reflecting its parent companies' home territory—Agfa in West Germany and Gevaert in Belgium.

These four companies stay abreast of each other's actions, and if one company makes a move, they can quickly respond to defend their home markets. Sakura increased the number of frames on a roll of film from 20 to 24, and was immediately copied by Fuji and Kodak in Japan and eventually by Kodak in the United States. Fuji's introduction of ASA 400 film was countered by the remaining three manufacturers within a few months worldwide. Even Kodak's epoch-making introduction of the disk camera was followed by Fuji and Sakura within one year. (Whether or not this new type of photography is really meeting the customers' needs is beside the point; the moves by Fuji and Sakura are simply intended to plug a potential hole in the dam to prevent future floods from competitors.) Kodak entered Polaroid's traditional territory of instant photography a decade ago. Because instant photography was not

---

* Thorn-EMI and Philips each has around 25 percent share in the United Kingdom.

an immediate success in Japan, Fuji waited and watched before introducing Fotorama, a very high-quality instant photography system. No sooner had Fuji announced the introduction of Fotorama, than Sakura tied up with Polaroid in Japan and started distributing Polaroid products against those of Kodak and Fuji. Again, no difference in the net position.

Today, all four companies have almost identical product lines, with each using its distribution and research strengths to neutralize the impact of its competitors' strategic moves. This is possible because amateur photography is an industry where the user end of the business system is of prime importance, namely the location of outlets to sell and develop film. Given the importance of outlets in Japan, even the most powerful new product cannot penetrate the market unless a company establishes access to the over 50,000 outlets (of which about 10,000 account for 70 percent of sales) and 600 film processing laboratories (which are mostly franchised and hence very expensive to build anew).

Despite Kodak's technological and overwhelming financial strengths, the other three companies have survived mainly because of their strengths at home. Today, these three companies have grown to the extent that they are attempting to tackle Kodak's home turf.

TRUE COMPETITORS

ALL OF THE TRUE WORLDWIDE COMPETITORS have already attained the status of domestic giants. Within Europe, European companies have become true, and most awesome, competitors. In Japan or in the United States, the situation is the same. Thus, in today's entrenched competitive world, all of the surviving companies are strong enough to withstand foreign invasions. On the other hand, it's only the strong domestic competitors who can wipe out a well-established corporation. Foreign companies can threaten, influence, and even inflict damage. But, as we will see in the case of Honda and Yamaha, even the giants can be quite vulnerable when they are attacked by their counterparts at home.

This is the case in one industry after another. One example is the electronics industry in Europe.

After a series of arguments back and forth, France's Thomson CSF takeover of Grundig, the ailing German consumer electronics company, did not materialize. Several months later Philips announced its acquisition of Grundig. In other words, a strong European company ended up devouring a weaker European company.

This is also the case in the automobile industry. In the

United States, both Ford and Chrysler are faced with threats from General Motors, particularly because GM has announced that it is splitting the company into two divisions, one specializing in large and the other in small cars. The big car GM division does not have to face Japanese competition, as the latter does not manufacture passenger cars with engines over 2,600 cc. Therefore, if GM's Large Car Division does well, it would be taking the share of the big car market away from Ford and Chrysler.

In the small car segment, the Big Three automakers have similar strengths and weaknesses. The Japanese Nine auto manufacturers (Toyota, Nissan, Honda, Toyo Kogyo–Mazda, Mitsubishi, Fuji Heavy Industries–Subaru, Isuzu, Suzuki, and Daihatsu) have similar strengths in terms of cost and performance. So, if GM's small car division concept works and uniquely improves its small cars to the extent that it can differentiate itself from Ford and Chrysler, both of these latter manufacturers will be affected before the Japanese Nine. In fact, if GM does so well as to affect the Japanese, the other two automobile manufacturers in Detroit will be severely affected.

Also, GM already holds a stake in three of the Japanese Nine, that is, in Isuzu, Suzuki, and now with Toyota. So, from these speculations, and from the analysis of the past share gains and losses of the Big Three, it is clear that the domestic titan GM is the true competitor of Ford and Chrysler.

The same situation is true in Japan. The across-the-board participants like Nissan, Mitsubishi, Toyo Kogyo, and Honda are all worried about Toyota. Conversely, Toyota worries about Nissan and Honda. Their relative share is reported in the newspaper every month, and we watch the race as if watching the Derby. Toyota also is worried about the second-tier companies, because each of them has unique strengths and weaknesses and could eat up a significant portion of Toyota's 33 percent share of Japanese market in a number of small bites.[1]

From the point of the remaining eight companies out of the Nine, tying up with foreign companies is better than being eaten alive by Toyota. So Nissan went ahead and agreed to distribute Volkswagen products in Japan, in exchange for production of one Nissan model in Wolfsburg. Mazda invited Ford's capital. The leader of the trend was Mitsubishi Motors, which tied up with Chrysler 15 years ago when it was separated from Mitsubishi Heavy Industries (MHI). Mitsubishi Heavy Industries at that time was concerned about its automobile division's future in competition against Toyota and Nissan, and rather than tying up with domestic competitors, MHI's president, the late Yoichiro Makita, chose Chrysler as its partner. It is well known that this alliance was helpful to Mitsubishi initially, but it was more advantageous to Chrysler through its economic crisis during the late 1970s and early 1980s. Although Chrysler was slow in downsizing its product lines, it was able to generate profits from sales of the Colt, Challenger, and Sapporo—all from Mitsubishi.

Likewise, Mazda (Toyo Kogyo) tied up with Ford when it was faced with a financial crisis in the mid-1970s, due mainly to the untimely introduction of the Wankel engine. When the Environmental Protection Agency (EPA) declared that this engine gulped gasoline, the post–oil shock consumers swung back to reciprocal engines. During the crisis, Mazda, with the help of Sumitomo Bank, chose to invite Ford's capital, rather than domestic foes.

Japan used to have 32 auto manufacturers. The number is now down to 11. Excluding the truck and bus specialists, there are nine passenger car producers. Of these nine, Subaru (Fuji Heavy Industries) forged the loose federation with Nissan, and Daihatsu with Toyota. But the remaining seven automakers are quite independent-minded. As a result of fighting the fierce battle at home and abroad, it seems to them that alliance with foreign capital is a more acceptable "disgrace" than the humiliation of surrender to their time-honored rivals.

The power of domestic competition can be seen in quite another industry in Japan. The toiletries industry is going through an interesting battle. It was triggered by Procter and Gamble (P&G), in an industry dominated by only two indigenous companies, Lion Oil and Fats and Kao Soap. The main

47

battlefield P&G chose initially was detergents. It acquired a small Japanese company, named San Home, and launched an all-out attack on the two companies. They retaliated, and every move by P&G in terms of price and product was matched. Through the process, P&G had accumulated some $125 million in losses in Japan.[2]

Having gone through this process, both Lion and Kao have realized that foreign invasion is something they can live with, but that in the end each company is the other's real competitor. Quite recently, and after surviving P&G's onslaught, Lion Oil and Fats merged with Lion Toothpaste to form Lion, Ltd. The stated intention of the merger, according to Atsushi Kobayashi, president of the new company, is to strengthen Lion Oil and Fats' traditional detergent business against the market leader, Kao.

Ever since this merger, these two companies have been competing head to head, matching each other's strategic and operational moves. Stated in other words, when the two domestic companies started this war, P&G had to be on defense. As Sun Tzu said, "Offense is the best defense": P&G has been locked into a stalemate situation in the Japanese domestic detergent market at about an 11.5 percent share for the past seven years.[3,4]

Both Kao and Lion might look for offshore alliances, but it looks quite clear this match will continue until one declares that it is defeated.

Perhaps the most striking example of how strong domestic competitors can harm each other comes from the motorcycle industry.[5] For many years, Honda and Yamaha were the major competitors in the motorcycle market in Japan. But when Honda assumed leadership in two-wheel vehicles, it also diversified into four-wheel vehicles. Yamaha Motors, on the other hand, specialized to a greater degree in the two-wheel variety and started gradually approaching Honda's market position. In 1970, Honda had more than a three-to-one lead over Yamaha in sales. But by 1979, Honda's motorcycle sales were leveling off, and Yamaha reduced Honda's lead to 1.4 to 1.

Yamaha then issued what amounted to a declaration of

war. At a conference in January 1982, the president of Yamaha Motors, Hisao Koike, told his most influential domestic dealers, "In a year, Yamaha shall occupy first place in the domestic market. Furthermore, two years from now, Yamaha shall be the world's top manufacturer of motorcycles." Eventually, word of Koike's declaration found its way to the offices of Honda executives.

Honda took up the challenge. In one year, Honda awed the market by offering 40 new models. To compete, Yamaha and Suzuki—the latter of which occupied the no. 3 position in the industry—manufactured more than 20 new models. As a result of the intense competition and the flood of new models, prices fell and some models actually sold for less than half of their actual cost.

The competition between Honda and Yamaha turned into a battle of financial staying power. Because Honda had the income from its automobiles, it had the advantage. But the impact of the battle was not clear for some time. Yamaha's financial results for the period ending April 30, 1982 showed record sales and profits.

But, later in 1982 the figures showed trouble, so Genichi Kawakami, chairman of Yamaha Motors, named a special team to find a solution to the red ink—a significant action because Kawakami had relied on Koike for decades. Then, beginning in March 1983, Kawakami—unaccompanied by aides—began visiting Japanese banks in search of loans. The new loans brought Yamaha Motor's total debt up to 220 billion yen, or one billion dollars.

The final chapter of the battle: Kawakami—president and CEO of Yamaha Motor's parent, Nippon Gakki, as well as Chairman of Yamaha Motors—took Koike to Kiyoshi Kawashima, president of Honda, and apologized for trying to overtake Honda. Then, at a press conference, the apology was repeated, and Kawakami announced Koike's dismissal.

When the battle was over, among the remaining debris were an estimated two million motorcycles. And rather than being assured of the no. 2 spot in the motorcycle industry, Yamaha had to take on Suzuki for that position.

The duel had been one of the bloodiest in recent history of the Japanese industrial scene. Why did Yamaha end up under a half-billion-dollar debt and under bank control? Why did it have to fight against Honda when their combined goal share was as high as 76 percent of the motorcycle market[6] and the two could have enjoyed the Pax Romana under the oligopoly? It all goes back to the reality that the true competitors are all domestic giants, and the "if we don't kill them, they will kill us" feeling.

The motorcycle industry is not an exception. Seiko and Citizen fight in timepieces. Canon and all other camera companies fight. Ricoh fights Canon in the field of plain paper copiers. Sharp and Casio do battle in pocket calculators. And everyone fights against Nippon Electric Company in microchips and computers.

PART III

THE SCORECARD OF GLOBAL COMPETITION

As we have just seen, many companies that are leaders in their industries at home are much less successful overseas. There are internal and external factors that inhibit or promote a company's success abroad. What has not been understood by the journalists and scholars who occasionally scan through the overseas newspapers is the psychological factors which are so deeply buried in the company's internal affairs that they do not surface on the balance sheet of the companies—until it is too late. Company officers are not interested in advertising the impotence of their own management.

When things start going wrong, these businesses avoid visitors, journalists, or mention of particular overseas subsidiaries, and send in "fire fighters" to control the situation. Rarely can these fire fighters arrest the situation. For most frequently, the very cause of the problem is people. It takes years to create a group of competent managers, who can address all key strategic and inside aspects of the business system with full knowledge of competitors and customers. Often the fire fighters, who are otherwise fine managers in domestic or corporate divisions where they are better supported by corporate staff, predictably start malfunctioning. They don't speak the

51

language, or the "right" language for a given time, place, and occasion. They are in such a hurry that they make decisions quicker than they listen to their own people. And they often rely on few—or no—advisers because they seldom have the time to get acquainted with the business and social leaders of the country. What they *can* do is "reduce," "cut," "prune," "remove," "stop," and "fire." Nothing is harder than the careful approach, a "soft landing" onto an ongoing organization, especially if it is a foreign one with a totally different corporate culture and physiology.

In the end, rather than acknowledging their own strategic blunders, the fire fighters who have been sent, as well as the corporate executives, start finding good excuses:

△ The competitors have natural (or "unfair") advantages.

△ Government regulations are too restrictive to foreigners and we suffer.

△ The fire fighter's predecessor allowed the employees to destroy each other (or go home at 4:30, it doesn't matter).

△ The company's product's FOB price is 20 percent higher than the competitor's shipment price.

△ The competitor's turnaround time (from design to mass production shipment) is only one third of the company's, and the firm's engineers are not very cooperative.

△ You can't get competent managers to work for a foreign subsidiary (or, if you hire managers who are too good, they will not put up with our corporate nonsense, or whatever!).

These excuses aside, the perception of a fire fighter—or any outsider, for that matter—of overseas business is different, depending on the outsider's perspectives. The most important thing for executives around the world is to know the reality, and then to establish their own viewpoint, devoid of prejudices. For prejudices often create passive and negative actions, and seldom produce positive and profitable results. In this context, I would like to debunk two of the most widely shared beliefs concerning the success and failure of global competitors.

1. Japan's successful international trade does not mean the Japanese are good managers overseas. There is no doubt that the Japanese can produce well at home, and export successfully. However, there is no evidence to date for asserting that the Japanese can successfully run a sizable company in OECD countries.

2. The Western countries' imbalance of trade with Japan does not mean they do poorly *in* Japan. In fact, most blue chip American and European companies are doing extremely well in Japan, either on their own like Nestle and IBM, or with a Japanese partner like Philips (with Matsushita Electric Industrial), Caterpillar (with Mitsubishi Heavy Industries), Honeywell (with Yamatake), and Xerox (with Fuji Film). As many strong American and European companies moved into Japan some time ago and established a full business system, the "trade," which is a measure of the flow of goods across the ocean, has shrunk. As most Japanese companies are still exporting, and many Western companies are producing in Japan, the imbalance has become large and difficult to manage. But the fact remains that there are many very successful insiders of foreign origin in Japan. These corporations are successful today because they have taken the time to do several critical things right, particularly in the area of developing local managers and relationships with business associates, such as vendors and distributors.

We can learn a great deal about the nature of the global business, especially the difficulty of doing business in the critical Triad markets away from home, by examining closely the following two puzzling questions:

53

△ Why can't the Japanese move into the United States and the European Community with a complete business system?

△ Why, despite obvious difficulties, have so many U.S. and European companies become insiders in Japan?

Now, let me take up each of these puzzles in the following two chapters.

JAPANESE COMPANIES
IN THE UNITED STATES
AND EUROPE

JAPAN'S MUCH-ACCLAIMED SUCCESS in the West and the resulting trade friction have been considerably exaggerated. An objective review of Japan's progress overseas reveals some interesting truths.

1. *Japan is not strong and competitive across the board.* Japan's secondary industry, its manufacturing and construction sectors, is important to the nation; it employs 34 percent of the working population. But more than two of three industries are not internationally competitive. These industries include basic and applied chemicals, pharmaceuticals, aerospace, processed foods, cement, aluminum, and pulp and paper, just to name a few. Japan is strong in industries corresponding to only 13 percent of its working population. These are basically hardware exporting industries, and hence they are quite visible to an ordinary man or woman. Furthermore, 56 percent of the population is engaged in service industries, which are not competitive (for example, distribution) or not export-oriented (for example, public services).

About 10 percent of Japan's working population is engaged in primary industries, of which only fishery is marginally competitive, and the rest are miserably uncompetitive. The

55

best example is agriculture, where Japanese productivity is only one third to one quarter that of the United States—though an apple-to-apple comparison would be impossible because of the differences in automation and the size of units of farming land. At any rate, Japan imported $6.3 billion of American agricultural products in 1983.[1] It was by far the biggest customer of American farmers, no. 2 being the Netherlands at only $2.6 billion.

Japan's primary industries, forestry, mining, and agriculture, are all subsidized by the government in one way or other, and are hardly competitive. Except for fisheries, Japanese primary industries, employing 10 percent of the population, are at the mercy of taxpayers' money, which is allocated to protect the "minimum national security," in case of a "food-OPEC"!

Now let us get back to my main arguments and recap some of the points: because Japan's major exports, for example, automobiles, consumer electronics, cameras, and watches, are so visible, the Western world has the false impression that all Japanese industries, and *therefore management*, are competitive and generally successful. In truth, the productivity of the Japanese retail industry is only 70 percent that of the United States. Japanese service industries, including banking, airlines, and insurance companies, follow the same trend in productivity. In addition, products of these industries are less suited for export. Conversely and ironically, the relatively greater efficiency of service industries (for example, distribution) in the United States has catalyzed the penetration of Japanese imports.

Only 24 percent of the population is engaged in manufacturing, excluding the 10 percent involved in construction. Here again, competitiveness is not uniform. For example, chemical and food industries are much smaller than their counterparts in the United States and the European Community. The biggest Japanese chemical companies have sales in the category of a few billion dollars; Mitsubishi Chemical has $3.6 billion in sales and Sumitomo $2.7 billion, as opposed to the $10 billion to $15 billion range for ICI, DuPont, BASF, Hoechst, and Bayer. Even the largest Japanese food company,

Yukijirushi, has about $3.2 billion in sales, as opposed to $6 billion to $13 billion for Nestle, General Foods, and Beatrice Foods, not to speak of Unilever at $22 billion. In addition, because Japan's constitution restricts rearmament, Japanese military and aerospace industries are infants compared with those of the United States, the United Kingdom, France, and West Germany.

In fact, Japanese spending on armaments and defense is only 1 percent of GNP, or approximately $10 billion, compared with the Soviet Union's $191 billion, the United States' $176 billion, West Germany's $29 billion, and Saudi Arabia's $24 billion. Japan's per capita defense spending ($89) is almost negligible. In fact, the R&D expenditure in the whole aerospace industry in Japan is not accurately calculated. For there is no such classification in the MITI's code similar to the American Standard Industrial Classification (SIC) Code. The reason is most Japanese aerospace companies are conglomerates, and their main businesses are heavy machinery, such as shipbuilding and power plants—for example, Mitsubishi Heavy Industries; automobiles—for example, Nissan; electronics—for example, Toshiba. So the scanty amount spent for defense R&D by these industries is certainly buried, or, more accurately, borne by other profitable businesses until the aerospace industry becomes more independent.

If we remove these uncompetitive industries from the manufacturing sector, the remaining (that is, competitive) industries correspond to only 13 percent of the Japanese working population. They are mainly assembly industries, characterized by mass production, with the possible exception of steelmaking. Thus, overall, Japan's "power" is limited to a few industries. This structural weakness of Japan, which has existed all along, is not well understood either by foreigners or by the Japanese. Japan is not a superstar. But it is not a failure, either. Like many other big nations, Japan has strengths and weaknesses, each for good reasons. What is important is to get beneath the journalistic overview and labels, and understand with a businessperson's objectivity what can be done about Japan's strengths and weaknesses.

2. *The remaining export potential of Japan's strong in-*

dustries is limited. I am not playing ambassador, but this is the unfortunate consequence of Japan's "success." In strong industries, Japan's production share in the world is already very high. For example, Japanese merchant shipbuilders have been responsible for approximately 50 percent of worldwide tonnage for the last 20 years. However, their share is not increasing and it is considered to be at the practical upper limit. The reasonable limit of penetration is observable in other areas: Japanese steel holds about 20 percent of the global share, significantly below that of the shipbuilding industry because steelmaking tends to be more indigenous to and dependent upon a national economy; television's 40 percent and semiconductors' 30 percent penetration of the global production share have already encountered trade restrictions.

Japanese automobile production accounted for approximately 30 percent of global output in 1983, and that is considered an upper limit for a nation whose population accounts for only 2.5 percent of that of the world.

Not surprisingly, trade frictions are significantly less if a product is relatively new, because the recipient country's labor force is not being displaced. For example, Japanese-produced electronic cash registers account for 80 percent of global production, Japanese high-fidelity equipment for 70 percent, Japanese VCRs for 95 percent, and Japanese handheld calculators for 60 percent of the world's production.

During 1981–1982, there was an uproar in France over imports of Japanese VCRs, today known as "the Second Battle of Poitiers." The French government shifted the customs examination from international ports to a small town in the middle of the country where Charles Martell stopped the Arab invasion in the original battle of Poitiers in 732 A.D. This naturally slowed down the customs process and the Japanese VCRs piled up in French ports of entry awaiting examination.

But a situation like this is rather rare. Because the Japanese imports were not displacing the existing labor force, the arguments were primarily based on the "opportunity loss," had the French made an equivalent amount of VCRs. What happened in France in the mean time was that the price of

the units doubled, and consumers at large became unsuppor-
tive of the French government's protectionist attitude. So
eventually in the middle of the following year, 1983, after a
series of serious governmental discussions and intermediary
roles played by the European Community's Trade Committee
representatives, the customs examinations were gradually
shifted away from Poitiers and a greater number of entrance
points were created, thus facilitating speedier entrance of the
Japanese VCRs into France. However, the aftermath of this
"battle" was, after all, a quota on the number of Japanese
VCR import at 430,000 units a year and the imposition of
an obligation to obtain prior approval of imports by the minister of French external trade.

Trade frictions in today's world are mainly caused and
sustained due to the existence of a powerful labor force whose
very being is threatened. This is the reason why Japanese
orange, rice, and beef markets have not been completely liber-
alized. If one asks average Japanese citizens what they would
like to see, they would undoubtedly say, "cheaper oranges,
rice, and beef [regardless of origin]." Often one mistakes the
voice of the government, being affected by strong lobbying
groups, for the general public's opinion, when one reads about
overseas events. Often these misleadings are the result of a
series of very clever bureaucratic manipulations of the public
opinion. But they seldom represent average consumer preferences, a point an objective businessperson should not overlook.

This is why industries where manufacturers are rather
fragmented and small in capitalization cause only modest
trade friction. Japanese motorcycles (68 percent of the global
production share), industrial sewing machines (70 percent),
and single lens cameras (80 percent) have not yet set off the
level of political and diplomatic problems witnessed by such
big industries as automobiles and color televisions.[2-4] The recent debate over charging 45 percent duty on motorcycles
imported into the United States to save the small but prestigious company of Harley-Davidson may not get popular
support from Americans, who have become avid buyers of
Hondas, Yamahas, Suzukis, and Kawasakis.

Interestingly enough, in the U.S. International Trade Commission's ruling on antidumping suits, we find a direct relationship to the three aforementioned parameters, namely, the growth rate of the industry, the number employed, and the profitability of American companies in the industry in question.[5]

Thus, it appears that Japan's remaining export potential is limited because of its already high share of the global market for exportable products, and because trade friction will further slow down export-based penetration of products that meet strong competition in Western countries.

3. *An overseas market is often "flooded" in anticipation of government quotas.* The tendency to flood a market became "established" with Japan's experience in exporting color televisions to the United States. In 1977, after long trade negotiations between the two countries, the Japanese color television manufacturers' association reluctantly accepted a quota on the number of sets to be shipped to the United States. The allotment of 1.56 million sets was then divided among individual manufacturers in proportion to their respective 1976 shipment record. As a result, those who boosted their export sales in 1976, the year before the quota, secured a relatively large allocation in 1977.

This experience has set a precedent; when there is a rumor that a country is considering a quota, the Japanese companies tend to flood that country's market. The 1980–1981 surge of color television exports to Europe and automobiles to the United States and to most European countries were the result of this psychological warfare among the Japanese competitors. While Japanese manufacturers, who usually ignore the guidance from the Ministry of International Trade and Industry and the Ministry of Foreign Affairs, dash to establish a favorable statistical record, their behavior raises an even greater outcry against the Japanese. This, in turn, accelerates government regulations. What causes this surge is a reflection on the sad nature of the Japanese managers who are preoccupied with having to beat their domestic competitors in order to survive.

Unfortunately, this phenomenon is viewed by the receiving countries as "Japan, Inc." marching in concert. In other words, tariffs force the Japanese to produce inside the Western marketplace, but quotas trigger the surge.

At any event, the net result of either of these two restrictive measures is higher prices for the consumer. After two years of automobile quotas restricting the number of Japanese cars entering the United States to 1.68 million units a year, Detroit's Big Three (Ford, Chrysler, and General Motors) all recovered miraculously. However, it is less known to the American public that the price American consumers paid for a Japanese car in 1983 was some 50 to 100 percent higher than a comparable car's price in Japan. Because the Japanese car companies made so much money on exports under the quota system, they reallocated their assets to gain the domestic Japanese market share, and the price there eroded significantly during 1983 and 1984.

Another way of stating this phenomenon is that the American consumers are subsidizing the Japanese consumer's purchase of a car. Unfortunately, industry associations, government bureaucrats, corporate executives, and the public all see the issue from different angles, and they don't see (or don't want to see) these forces at work well enough to resolve the trade issues in a truly sophisticated way.

Perhaps the only exception has been the gentleman's agreement on the "trigger price" in the steelmaking industry. The Japanese steel industry takes pride and prestige in being no. 1 in the world. Japanese steel industry executives are also highly respected. Therefore they agreed in the late 1970s on a certain formula to follow to allow the American steelmaking industry to recover. However, the net result was that more European steel was imported to the United States. The lesson learned was that for this kind of agreement to be effective, it must be trilateral and must encompass the entire Triad. In the case of steel, it will have to encompass "Tetrahedron" regions, including such countries as Korea (for Japan) and Brazil (for the United States).

4. *As Japan's home market becomes more attractive, less*

emphasis will be placed on exports. The second energy crisis and the resultant depression in Japanese domestic consumption spurred Japan's export drive in the early 1980s. During the 1970s, consumer spending in Japan declined steadily with a greater portion of income going to savings and toward paying off housing-related long-term debts. Japanese spending on consumer durables dropped, especially for consumer electronic goods, automobiles, and musical instruments. As a result, manufacturers of these products vigorously sought out every possible overseas market. Furthermore, the favorable dollar–yen exchange rate made exports very attractive.

The economic recovery in the United States in 1983, one year ahead of that in Japan, further accelerated this trend, and the United States trade deficit with Japan reached an all-time high of $18 billion. However, Japan does represent a large and attractive market, and, as replacement demand for consumer durables such as refrigerators and televisions comes back and the yen strengthens, exports will become less attractive.

In the contemporary economy of the Triad nations, it is absolutely necessary to separate the problems of trade from those of currency. If the yen weakens, exporting Japanese goods to the United States will become attractive and easier. But then Japanese investors will start buying dollar-based bonds and securities. In fact, during 1983, Japanese investments in the United States reached levels on the order of $20 billion, and therefore the net flow of money was balanced. If the yen becomes stronger, this flow of money will reverse in direction and again move so as to compensate for the "real" trade balance.

However, even if the same amount of goods flow in physical quantities, and hence the same amount of "yen" is exported, it means more "dollars" with a stronger yen. Statistically, this situation creates a further imbalance of "trade," as expressed in dollars. One of the most urgent priorities in these trade-related debates is to develop an equation to express such terms as "balance," "fair," "closed," and "strong."

We spend a lot of time expressing our emotions across the borders of the Triad areas, but very little intellectual effort has been made to create the tools to resolve them. As we will observe in Chapter 8, no industrial classification system exists between the United States and Japan, let alone statistical and economic figures which would enable the two countries to be compared. This is even more true as regards Japan and Europe, where the statistical data are hard to come by to begin with. When Americans say "machine tools," the Japanese are thinking only about a dozen specific types of machinery. When the Japanese say "robots," they include simple "pick-and-place" manipulators because firms that install "robots" get a tax benefit on depreciation in Japan.

So one thing is for sure. We don't really have a good basis for becoming emotional. A true businessperson operating as an insider in each of the Triad regions must stay objective and address the fundamental issue of universal consumer needs and the major changes in the infrastructure such as communication and transportation networks and educational systems.

5. *Overseas manufacturing companies and facilities acquired by the Japanese often run into serious problems.* Of the 11 significant acquisitions in the United States made by the Japanese from 1973 to 1979, as many as 8 were troubled companies. This is in marked contrast to the acquisition of U.S. companies by the West Germans and the French, who typically buy profitable ventures.

Mergers and acquisitions are rare in Japan, and when one occurs it is almost always a rescue operation. Thus, it is a natural tendency of Japanese managers to assume that profitable companies are not "for sale." Additionally and importantly, Japanese experience with merger and acquisition is very limited; in the United States, from 1974 to 1978, the Japanese made only 47 acquisitions, or 5 percent of the total 876 mergers and acquisitions made by foreign companies.

Furthermore, Japanese acquisition techniques are not sophisticated. Nine out of ten firms are brought into the Japanese company by investment banks and/or trading companies, rather than the buyer making formal survey of interesting candidates. Since the buyers don't study the situation in depth and leave everything to the go-between dealers, the price tag can vary by a factor of 10 when a firm buys the same kind of company in the same industry, as was the case of the color television plants purchased by the Japanese in the United States.

Acquisitions are extremely strategic moves. If a competitor is rumored to be acquiring an American company, then it is more likely that the CEO of a company in the same industry will also demand a study of similar possibilities. Then, two things may happen. First, CEOs and their associates may lose their cool and objectivity, and the whole purpose of the study may become buying one particular company, rather than assessing whether such a move makes sense. Second, an acquisition normally requires such confidentiality that the task force leader and the CEO may handle the analyses and evaluation with little counseling from others in the company's top ranks. This creates a huge problem later because of lack of general support during the on-going process of running the acquired company.

Unlike other issues in Japan, where consensus gets the upper hand over analysis and dogmatic decision-making, decisions on acquisition are normally made behind closed doors by a few select persons, leaving everyone else in the dark. Thus, the acquired company, usually lacking resources and any other ammunition, further faces tacit neglect and lack of support from the bulk of the parent company. Therefore, the probability of success, from the onset, is usually very small.

6. *Most Japanese acquisitions in the West are aimed at securing production facilities against anticipated quotas and import restrictions.* These acquisitions face two fundamental problems. The first is that the acquired company is usually not competitive and its facilities are normally old and have not benefited from upgrading investment for a long time. That is usually the very reason for restrictions against the more competitive Japanese imports. What the acquirer buys is not much more than a piece of land, workers and manage-

ment, and obsolete inventories and equipment. Furthermore, most of these are small companies, except for a few banks on the United States' West Coast. As a result, if the acquirer cannot keep the atmosphere of the acquired company challenging and exciting, good employees leave, and what the acquiring firm is left with is only the acquired company's logo. Turning around this kind of situation is a very expensive task.

The second problem is the difference in production philosophy. Japanese manufacturers at home can get the full benefit of their country's rich resources, ranging from competent and flexible component suppliers to a subcontracted labor force. In comparison, U.S. and European companies tend to be more vertically integrated, and the supporting infrastructure is very different. It takes several years for Japanese management to fully understand these differences and begin to constructively lead their American and European operations. However, because the philosophical and practical gaps are so big, the needed leadership rarely develops. It is no wonder that companies like Sony, Yoshida Kogyo Kabushiki Kaisha (YKK), and Honda are cited as successful operators of their overseas plants. They do not acquire. They usually build their own plants on bare land, use their own layout and production philosophy, and train people to fit into their time-honored system.

A startling fact emerges from the study of successful Japanese operations overseas: all of them have been operated by one or two individuals for over a decade, if not a few decades. Except for financial and trading institutions, I don't know of any successful Japanese multinationals that operate as institutions. The most successful multinationals have been those whose corporate culture can be explained by the activities of one entrepreneur.

Take Matsushita, for example. Its founder Konosuke Matsushita has been at his job for a half century. But throughout Konosuke Matsushita's reign, Arataro Takahashi has consistently been in charge of overseas business, for at least 25 years as the chairperson of its trading company, Matsushita Electric Trading. Sanyo, whose founder, Toshio Iue, used to work for Matsushita and established his company in April 1950, named

65

his company Sanyo (Three Oceans) because he never thought he could beat Matsushita at home in Japan. At Sanyo, Emou Kamuro, now executive vice-president of its trading company, started a section to handle exports in September 1951, and Kamuro has been at it ever since.

Sony's first president in the United States was Akio Morita. To date, 38 years after its formation, Morita has crossed the Pacific over 300 times,[6] and has been the prime mover of Sony's overseas operations all along, and also of domestic operations since 1972.

Soichiro Honda's aspiration to become global dates back to 1948, when he was a subcontractor to Toyota and delivered a pep talk to his 25 employees. His lifetime aide, Michihiro Nishida recalls Honda standing up on a tangerine box and declaring that his company would someday become global.

Why is a motivating individual needed to build a global organization? The answer is very simple. Each subsidiary, with its full business system, is an independent company. It takes as much effort and entrepreneurship to make an overseas subsidiary viable as to create a new company. That means hiring and developing key members. That means building a coherent set of management processes, ranging from accounting to logistics. In order to hire a competent local manager, that person must be given a certain assurance of employment. The parent company can't hire and fire. On the other hand, it can't afford to let old and not-so-competent managers hang on for too long. For, if a company keeps managers who were hired when the subsidiary was small and insignificant, it will lose young and aggressive people quickly, or else the old folks may show them "bad corporate habits." A good manager overseas cannot be hired by an abstract entity called an "institution."

It takes an Akio Morita to hire (and fire) a Harvey Shein, Sony America's ex-CEO. A domestically oriented blue chip company with hopes of becoming global might use a head hunter to recruit a competent American general manager. Such a person might meet all the mechanical specifications developed by the corporate staff. But, in a few years' time, another general manager may be appointed to head the international division. The new general manager may not like the American general manager. Maybe it's their "chemistry." So the new international division's general manager hires the head hunter again, and looks for another suitable American general manager. In a few years' time, the same cycle is repeated again, which only comes to make the recruiting companies rich. Over the years, however, these subsidiary heads do not build the company's critical infrastructure, and above all, its human resources. They might reduce the inventory, and make a few critical and heroic sales to a few key accounts.

So after a decade of "ardent" effort, the main company is left with a noncompany. None of the critical seven S's of management,* shared values, strategy, style, skills, staff, structure, and systems, will be applied in an orderly fashion. If the same individual stays to oversee the most critical aspects of overseas operations, particularly those of people and systems development, then the company has a pretty good chance of building on its mistakes and experience. This is the reason why so often we see the entrepreneurial, but not institutional, success of overseas business.

Unfortunately for Japanese companies, by the time most of them realized that they cannot rely on trading companies to export and that they themselves must establish a full business system abroad, particularly in North America and Europe, these overseas operations had become sizable "establishments" themselves. Many of the Japanese companies approached these tough overseas markets institutionally with the full benefit of their corporate bureaucracy, and they failed in 100 of the 107 cases during the past decade.

7. *The Japanese cannot easily expand their operations in the West because of the lack in management talent.* Traditionally Japanese banks and trading houses have been internationalized to compensate for the lack of internationalization of the Japanese manufacturing sector. Even after manufacturers

---

* This refers to a framework developed by the McKinsey Development Project which eventually led to *In Search of Excellence*, by Thomas J. Peters and Robert H. Waterman, Jr., published by Harper & Row, New York, 1982.

have begun marketing overseas on their own, they rely heavily on the distributors and dealers of the host countries. However, direct manufacturing in the United States and Europe requires that management itself be internationalized. In addition to the top management functions, domestically oriented functions such as engineering, purchasing, production technology, and scheduling must be conducted in the host country.

Japanese companies do not have managers with the broad experience needed to oversee those functions at offshore (out-of-Japan) locations. Because of the nature of the work, managers for overseas operations are usually in their mid-thirties and forties. However, in a large Japanese company, professionals in this age bracket are specialists who lack general management experience, mastery of a foreign language, and other international business training.

The very technical nature of today's business world has brought forth specialists. In manufacturing, a leader must know a lot about plant layout, purchasing machine tools, and physical distribution. Today production engineers in their mid-thirties specialize in certain aspects of numerical control (NC) machines, for example. It takes a long time to become a true expert in any field of specialization. Twenty years ago when these companies grew domestically, most of the key managers were young and generalists. Now, the generalist age bracket has been pushed up to the mid-fifties, too old to go overseas and lead the whole production operations for ten years. Besides, these people dry up in a few days without raw fish and soy sauce, or without reading the *Asahi Shinbun* and watching the Yomiuri Giants ballgames on television during summer evenings.

So this dilemma is escalating. In order to manage a foreign operation with the full business system, you have to send out managers with solid generalist talents, at least initially until the foreign unit starts operating smoothly. In successful Japanese industries, where companies have become too established, we don't have these generalist talents in managers young enough to go abroad and live comfortably for ten years, the minimum time needed to assimilate a new corporate culture and modus operandi. In trading-houses and banks, career-path programming is very different, and specialists are trained to engage in international businesses. In fact, many of the leading financial institutions and trading-houses in Japan send dozens of students off every year to obtain advanced degrees in the United States and Europe. This is not true for manufacturers. And because it is the Japanese tradition not to recruit people from outside, the lack of international management talent is a serious and continuing problem.

Last, but not less important than the lack of talent for overseas business, is the unwillingness of Japanese managers to live abroad. Because of the affluence, good educational system, and safe urban and suburban life in Japan, most Japanese managers in their thirties and forties opt for staying at home. Two decades ago, it was a sign of recognition to be appointed a manager of overseas operations. Today, when a manager is sounded out by his or her boss on the possibility of moving overseas, the manager would find a dozen excuses why he or she would not be the best candidate for the position.

8. *Japanese management is not portable.* Adding to this problem is the absence of codified management systems. Because of the Japanese flexible organizational concept and the informal relationships between functions, on the one hand, and vendors and subcontractors, on the other, little of the Japanese management system is codified and systematized. Lifetime employment has enabled Japanese manufacturers to pass on the "secrets and know-how" to the next generation with a minimum amount of codification. This is a strength in Japan, but it is a tremendous hindrance for manufacturing operations overseas, especially in the West where culture, value systems, and other intangibles are so dramatically different from Japan.

In the 1950s and 1960s, when the Japanese were learning from the West about steelmaking, shipbuilding, power generation, semiconductors, and home appliances, a typical Japanese engineer was described as being short, wearing glasses, and carrying a camera. This image was, in reality, not too far off. These engineers, actually writers for the Japanese engineering corporations, traveled around the world and, with their voracious appetites, picked up knowledge of Western production systems and the latest technologies.

Back then, the Japanese manufacturers were known as copiers and they were generally looked down upon as making rather low quality, "me-too" products. However, these traveling engineers were smart, and played a crucial role in reforming the old-fashioned Japanese industrial system into a very competitive, global industrial power. Typically, they would write a lengthy report on their trip, spelling out what they saw and what they thought were the implications for their company. The report would be read and discussed, and often a special task force would be set up to implement such things as "NC-ization," "continuous casting," "large-scale blast furnaces," "zero-defects," "flex-time," and so forth.

Because of the high level of attention and visibility of the *Shutcho Hokoku* (business trip report), the traveling engineers were anxious to get any information to be incorporated in their Hokoku. This overzealous attitude to get new information was largely due to the role the travelers were likely to assume upon their return to Japan. And that was to head up the task force, to reproduce the most advanced system they saw in the West, and eventually to use those accomplishments to win promotion to a top position. The *Hokoku-kai* (reporting meeting) was attended by curious colleagues, as their compatriots had gathered to watch Francis Xavier, the Portuguese Catholic priest, talk about the guns on the Japanese island of Tanegashima in 1549, and to witness Commodore Perry in the Strait of Uraga in 1853.

The traveling Japanese engineers typically were generalists. They single-handedly picked up information on machinery, purchasing, logistics, plant layout, workers' participation, organization, finance, and even marketing. The point is, during those years, the traveling engineers were writing down and codifying information from other countries—not from Japan.

And they took pride in it. I recall a prominent executive telling me the European experience he was most proud of.

He said, "Back in 1960, I visited this gas turbine plant. The chief engineer proudly spread out very detailed blueprints of their latest product, and explained the unique technological features of the model. So I asked him to give me a copy of the blueprint, but he laughed and said 'You won't need it for a decade.' So I went back to the hotel, and spent the whole evening recollecting every detail of the design, and by dawn, I had the entire turbine reproduced!"

Having been a nuclear engineer and having created quite a few patents myself, I didn't think the executive's brag to me impressive or funny. But his points are well taken. In the old days, a supergeneralist Japanese engineer traveled around the world with a voracious appetite for everything new. And when there was something interesting, single individuals could reproduce what Western firms were doing when they returned to their home plants in Japan.

Currently the situation is reversed in many industries. The Japanese must show others how to do it. As in steelmaking, automobile making, and shipbuilding, the Japanese are not secretive. They invite both Western and Asian friends and show them their designs and their production and fabrication processes. However, the learners' appetite is in question. Very few of them come to visit the Japanese plant with the will to copy or reproduce. The Japanese are not good teachers either. They don't have well-documented manuals in either English or Japanese, nor do they have "experts" articulate enough to explain how the whole system works.

Those limitations as teachers will soon be clear. When Honda signed up to help British Leyland (BL), says one top Honda executive, the Honda team expected BL to send in a few design engineers and foremen. They did. But the BL contingent claimed that each BL employee's territory was so limited, they could not learn the whole system. Nor were the BL people allowed to learn it, because of the compartmentalized British unions. In the end, Honda ended up inviting three hundred foremen and engineers to Japan, many with their wives and children.[7] The amount of effort spent in this "transfer of know-how" process was, according to their executive, over one hundred times more than they had been prepared for.

Learning from Honda's experience, and reflecting on its own previous examples, Nissan built a dormitory in Kyushu for its American engineers and floor managers in preparation for the construction of its Tennessee plant in 1982–1983. Nissan's U.S. plant went into production in October of 1983, after some 270 American workers had been sent to Japan and trained hands-on for as long as three months to a half-year each.[8]

These examples indicate the difficulties of transferring Japanese management know-how to other countries, particularly to the unionized Western countries. It seems to me that the problem stems from a complex set of differences ranging from the infrastructure of the work force to the inability of most Japanese companies to crystallize and codify their know-how so that it is transportable.

Very few Japanese companies can afford the effort made by Honda and Nissan. So the success of a handful of these truly outstanding Japanese corporations should not be generalized too casually.

9. *Headquarters still smells like soy sauce.* Most executives in Japan come from domestic locations such as *gemba* (where the action is), be it in the sales or manufacturing operations. They keep this affinity to their *gemba* for their entire lives. This means they frequently talk on the phone with, or even visit, dealers, customers, vendors, and subcontractors. These people are all related to domestic operations. If the domestic market share of an executive's product declines, the executive is yelled at, and the company is visited by the press to find out the reason why this happened. If the shipment of products is slow in a bullish economy, executives get phone calls from all over the country. The executives pay attention.

Overseas, business is different. The dissatisfaction of customers and dealers reaches Japan via telex and written reports, and even most of the messages reach the headquarters' managers in charge of overseas businesses, not the CEO. Only 30 percent of the top 1,000 Japanese companies have a single manager in charge of overseas business who is above the managing director level. That's already three levels down from the CEO. Most Japanese corporations have a group of "foreign" specialists in the overseas division. This is a group of English-speaking individuals who used to write letters of credit (LOC) for trading companies. I call them "LOC-based foreign villagers." They usually have very limited experience in working deeply in the domestic *gemba*. They are certainly the specialists in terms of overseas business, but they seldom know how things work at home.

This separation of geographic competence worked fine when everything was designed and produced in Japan to be exported to overseas markets. But as more and more components of the entire business system were transferred overseas, particularly inside the Western markets, more managers had to learn the entire business system in a hurry. Some "LOC-based villagers" have managed to give the impression to the top executives that they indeed have made the transition successfully.

At any rate, the judges, that is, the top executives, also lack the qualification to be objective and informed judges, and their deficiencies have gone too far for too long without being fully recognized. Thus, in most Japanese companies, the foreign operation is not fully integrated with the critical functions of corporate staff and with the domestic operating divisions.

Usually the managers in charge of foreign operations are still left alone, without benefiting from the full support of the corporation's personnel, financial, and technical staffs. Neither the domestic nor the international side can see the other side and sketch out the overall picture. "Overseas villagers" have developed the habit of yelling when corporate resources are needed, but they usually prefer to be left alone, rather than being inspected and kicked around by the otherwise domestic-oriented corporate staffers.

Operating divisions that usually have global product responsibilities give priority in allocating engineering and manufacturing resources to their domestic operations. When their U.S. manufacturing operation is faced with start-up problems, they typically send second-rate managers who do what they are told to do and who seldom innovate. When their European operations face a low-utilization problem, they seldom shift the production mix away from home because they "don't know what to do with the excess workers at home."

Most Japanese corporations are still organized both at headquarters as well as at the operating division level to serve their domestic market well. That is why it sounded so refreshing when Dr. Koji Kobayashi, the chairman of NEC, said, "The United States is our second domestic market," and reorganized NEC accordingly. Honda does not have such divisions labeled domestic and overseas; it has marketing and sales divisions no. 1, no. 2, and no. 3, corresponding to Japan, the United States, and Europe, respectively. Hence, production plants and corporate functions are not distinguished one from the other. They are there to serve their respective divisions' needs equally well.

Other Japanese leaders also favor the United States. Sony has always treated the U.S. market better than Japan and has sent its top-quality people to manage its U.S. operations, including Akio Morita, the current chairman. Matsushita treats the United States differently from the rest of the world. While Matsushita Electric Trading in general is responsible for its overseas operations, Matsushita Electric Industrial, its parent and the manufacturing company, is directly responsible for the United States. The American operation, called Matsushita Electric Corporation of America (MECA) and headquartered in New Jersey, recorded $3 billion in sales in 1983 in the United States alone through its Panasonic, Quasar, and Technics businesses. This is bigger than Zenith, at $1.2 billion (in 1982),[9] Matsushita's traditional competitor in the United States.

Thus, successful Japanese companies are organized to be successful. However, these are few and far between, and we have a large number of corporations that are still organized to export, and not organized to run business systems as insiders in the advanced regions of the United States and the European Community.

In summary, I do not anticipate the Japanese manufactur-

74

ers to move a significant portion of their business system directly into the United States and Europe. There will also be very limited acquisitions of American and European companies by the Japanese, except in high-technology and financial industries. It will be a long time before Japanese management acquires the capabilities, both in terms of organizational skills and personnel, to run a sizable corporation with a full business system either in the United States or in the European Community. Such complete operations should be distinguished from the numerous convenience units which are likely to be set up to avoid and/or overcome various types of import restrictions.

In this chapter I have reviewed the reasons why even blue chip Japanese companies are having difficulties in establishing a complete business system in key OECD markets. Although I am not an expert on American corporations in Europe and on European companies in the United States, similar difficulties have been observed by many of my colleagues.* I would now like to discuss the position of American and European firms in Japan.

---

* My McKinsey colleagues, Herbert Henzler in Munich and Tino Puri and Chuck Farr in New York, are developing both a data base and case histories on European and American multinationals.

8

U.S. AND EUROPEAN COMPANIES IN JAPAN

JUST AS JAPAN'S SUCCESS in the West has been exaggerated, so too has American and European companies' lack of success in Japan. I recently directed a study co-sponsored by the United States–Japan Trade Study Group (TSG) and McKinsey & Company. Published under the title *Japan Business: Obstacles and Opportunities*, the study concluded that many, though not all, of the obstacles to success in Japan are perceived rather than real, and that business activity by the foreign-affiliated companies in Japan is actually considerable. "Because we hear so many horror stories, we needlessly discourage foreign investors to Japan," says Faneuil Adams, former Chairman of Mobil Sekiyu, who was one of the steering committee members of the TSG study.

Western countries' imbalance of trade with Japan does not mean they do poorly *in* Japan. In fact, most blue chip American and European companies are doing extremely well

Note: A portion of the data contained in Chapter 8 is based on a project co-sponsored by the United States–Japan Trade Study Group and McKinsey & Company. Its findings were published in *Japan Business: Obstacles and Opportunities* (distributed in the United States by John Wiley & Sons, New York, 1983).

in Japan, either on their own, like Nestle and IBM, or with a Japanese partner, like Philips (with Matsushita Electric Industrial), General Foods (with Ajinomoto), or Xerox (with Fuji Film). Because most potent American and European companies moved into Japan some decades ago and established a full business system, the "trade"—which is a measure of the flow of goods across the ocean—has shrunk. Since most Japanese companies are still exporting, and many Western companies are producing in Japan, the trade imbalance has become large and difficult to manage.

But the fact remains. That is, unlike the widely perceived notion that Japan is a closed market and difficult for foreign companies, there are many very successful insiders of foreign origin in Japan. These corporations are successful today because they have taken the time to do several critical things right, particularly in the area of developing local managers and relationships with business associates such as vendors and distributors.

Now let me expand on our TSG findings to illustrate these points with as many facts as I can incorporate. Also, by presenting the fruit of our interviews and studies, the factors for succeeding in a tough foreign market, regardless of the host country, will hopefully emerge. Because insiderization in Japan has been perceived to be most difficult for U.S. and European corporations, I will elaborate on the perception and the management issues in as much detail as possible in this chapter.

Level of Activity

1. *The total U.S. export volume to Japan is greater than is generally known.* The focus on the deficit in goods traded, a record $7.8 billion[1] in the first quarter of 1984, overshadows the substantial inroads American goods have made in the Japanese marketplace, both in value and in variety. Literally thousands of U.S. companies are marketing products in Japan either directly or through agents. According to U.S. Embassy

statistics, more than 5,000 agents in Japan are offering U.S. goods. A conservative projection of ten products per agent gives some indication of the range of U.S. products—around 50,000—currently available in Japan. In services, the U.S. lead was between $1.9 and $3.4 billion in 1980, according to the U.S. and Japanese data bases, respectively. Regardless of the difference in data, the overall picture remains the same: over the past decade, U.S. service exports to Japan, for example, banks and airlines, grew at a rate equal to or higher than Japanese service exports to the United States.

Fees and royalties from technological agreements, which are included under services, represent one of the most used forms of participation in Japan by U.S. firms. In fact, as we will see later, most American consumer packaged goods companies choose to license brands and know-how to the Japanese rather than establish their own operations. U.S. Commerce Department data show that licensing receipts from Japan were $809 million in 1980, reflecting a growth of 22.1 percent per year since the 1970s. American companies account for about 50 percent of the large volume of technological agreements with Japan, nearly half of them in areas where Japan has now taken a leading position.

Other royalty-rich market sectors include proprietary soft drink concentrates, records, fast food, printed materials, and motion picture films. Japan, for example, represents about 10 percent of overseas rentals to U.S. filmmakers. Conversely, very few Japanese films are shown in the United States.

Theoretically, assuming licensing fees to be between 1 and 4 percent of sales, equivalent sales of U.S. goods in Japan would be $10 to $60 billion, providing a dramatically different picture of the balance of trade between the two nations today. Thus, in the long run licensing can have a significant negative impact on trade balance statistics, which reflect only goods transported between the two countries.

Less theoretical and far more concrete, however, is the value of goods and services and tangible products not captured in bilateral trade statistics. To illustrate, in the service sector repatriated profits on overseas banking operations are reflected in trade statistics. Regarding tangible products, in 1980 U.S. firms shipped $21 billion in crude oil to Japan from Third World countries and the associated profits were not reflected in United States/Japan bilateral trade statistics. This is one of the reasons why some Japanese argue that Japan should ask the major American firms to take Middle East oil to the United States and ship Alaskan oil to Japan. Statistically, this will wipe out the reported trade imbalance between Japan and the United States of approximately $20 billion in 1983. Needless to say, this exercise will further worsen the U.S. trade imbalance with the OPEC nations.

2. *The depth of penetration of U.S. exports into the Japanese market is greater than generally perceived.* American penetration into Japanese manufacturing sectors has been less obvious than Japan's penetration into America's, but it has encompassed a wider range of industries. Although many U.S. exports to Japan are in the primary sector (agricultural and mining goods), American inroads into Japan have not been limited to this sector. Japan is America's number one foreign purchaser of commercial aircraft, organic and inorganic chemicals, pharmaceuticals, and photographic supplies. It is the second largest foreign purchaser of medical and scientific supplies, measuring and testing devices, pulp and wood products, and semiconductors.

American politicians are very smart in talking about the trade issues with the Japanese. They say Japan should "open" the market, thereby implying it is currently closed. For example, Japan imported $5.6 billion in American agricultural products in 1982 and was by far the biggest customer of American farmers. And this includes such "closed" products as oranges and beef!

The trouble is twofold. First, because these products are not visible to average consumers, they never question their origin. For example, who would ask where the beef comes from when one eats teriyaki steak in Tokyo? Second, American people in general do not take great pride in being the strongest and most productive agricultural nation, but they are rather visibly disappointed in not being so competitive in automobiles and color televisions. When Japan and the United States get together to discuss the trade issues these days, they get excited about oranges and beef. The U.S. representatives ask to "open" the market. A more accurate expression would be to "enlarge the quota."

For already in 1982, even before "opening" the market, Japan was buying 64 percent of U.S. beef and veal exports, or $234 million, and 26 percent of U.S. orange and tangerine exports, or $51 million, not to speak of a half of the $100 million in U.S. grapefruit exports. In general, an average of 15 to 30 percent of American agricultural exports are absorbed by the Japanese, ranging from feed grains, corn, soybeans, cotton, and tobacco to wheat and soybeans. So, if Japan imports more beef, it will affect the noncompetitive domestic cattle growers, which will certainly force them to reduce the purchase of imported corn (currently $1.5 billion from the United States) and/or the $1.6 billion of feed grain imported from the United States. Japanese cattle grow almost exclusively on U.S. feedstocks.

The point here is that Japan's agriculture, including what is grown and raised in Japan, is totally dependent on the United States. It makes very little difference to the trade balance in what form the Japanese buy from the United States, unless, of course, the Japanese diet structure dramatically alters. It will be up to the U.S. farmers to decide whether exporting beef is better than exporting corn and feed grains.

A similar case in point is tobacco. Because tobacco is one of the most critical sources of tax revenue, the Japanese have allowed the government to monopolize the tobacco and salt businesses. Recently, pressure from the United States has been aimed at liberalizing cigarette sales in Japan, as symbolic signs of opening up the "closed market" to the Americans. Here again, the dilemma—similar to the corn and beef issue—exists. The Japanese government monopoly imported as much as $338 million in tobacco from the United States in 1983. This corresponds to approximately 23 percent of the total amount of tobacco leaves exported by U.S. farmers. This means that even if Japan switched to importing American cigarettes instead of tobacco the net trade flow would not improve dramatically. In other words, even if this industry were to be converted to free competition, the Japanese will not see a major difference in trade statistics.

It is simply a question of the United States deciding what is socially acceptable. That is, do the American people want to support the cigarette companies or is it sufficient that the tobacco growers are happy? The latter obviously are today because they sell so much to the Japanese, at favorable prices. One thing for sure is that the Japanese are not going to smoke more, regardless of the (resultant) tobacco companies' heated competition. The cigarette industry in Japan, as is the case in the United States, is a declining one and among adult Japanese males particularly cigarette smoking is declining rapidly.

The purpose of this section is not to expand the arguments about Japan–United States trade relationships, but rather to put the whole issue in perspective. Most international disputes are created and accelerated because each nation adopts a certain tone. Politicians and journalists, either knowingly or carelessly, tend to manipulate public sentiment and psychological dynamics for their immediate short-term advantage. Global businesspeople, particularly those who want to take advantage of the lucrative Triad potential, should not be bothered by this public posturing, and should be in a truly "insider" position, thus remaining objective, and should develop or keep an informed perspective on what is really happening, and what can really be turned to business advantage.

3. *The number and size of sales and manufacturing facilities are large.* Of the 1,968 foreign affiliated companies (FACs) operating in Japan in 1981, 671—or 34 percent—were American. [The Ministry of International Trade and Industry's (MITI) definition of a FAC is one with 25 percent foreign participation. The actual equity norm is closer to 50 percent.] A sampling of a significant portion of the FACs reveals that America's ratio of participation parallels that of other FACs across many major industry categories and is not concentrated in primary or resource-rich sectors, as is often believed. Of the approximately 700 FACs for which market rankings could

81

be identified, 85 percent of FACs ranked themselves among the top ten of their respective industry sectors. American firms accounted for more than half of the top-performing FACs. It should be noted that, overall, FACs performed better in terms of return on assets (ROA) (that is, 6 percent) than did their Japanese counterparts with an average of 3 percent ROA.

This could be explained in two ways. One is that only truly competitive U.S. and European companies come into Japan. However, we are talking about the average of approximately 2,000 FACs. It must therefore be interpreted as a more general phenomenon. Japan, once a firm establishes an insider position, is indeed not too bad a location in terms of growth and profitability. The second reason behind this rather high ROA is the influence of headquarters' guidelines. As we will further discuss in the section on "Internal Inhibitors" below, many FACs have imposed rather stringent profitability or return measures from the early days of operations in Japan. This tends to raise the participants' ROA, but often restricts their healthy growth. European companies, particularly West German ones, exercise this kind of numerical measures less than the Americans, although many of them set long-term growth and penetration targets in Japan.

America's direct investments in Japan far exceed those of any other country, but its rate of investment growth has slowed and no longer represents an overwhelming share of the total. In 1982, America's investment in Japan was about 3 percent of its total offshore investments of $221,343 million, according to U.S. Department of Commerce statistics. Despite the potential and despite the proven profits, U.S. direct investment abroad was the same in Japan as it was in Belgium, which had a gross domestic product (GDP) of $85 billion—a little less than one tenth of Japan's GDP of $1,060 billion. In fact, America's investment was 4.5 times greater in the United Kingdom, which had half the GDP of Japan. Even West Germany and France, whose GDPs were almost 40 percent and 50 percent less than Japan's, received 7 percent and 4 percent of America's investment, respectively. The Netherlands and Switzerland, whose combined GDPs represented less than one quarter of Japan's economic size, received more U.S. investment individually than did Japan.

Despite the slowing down of investment, Americans produce some $20 billion worth of goods via their subsidiaries or affiliates in Japan. Since the comparable figure for the Japanese in the United States was only $5.1 billion in 1981, the imbalance of production was $15 billion. These products are mostly consumed within the country of production, so they do not show up in the bilateral trade statistics. But they are certainly reflective of one country's ability to penetrate the other's market. In other words, in terms of the direct production by the multinationals, U.S. penetration in Japan is four times that of the Japanese in the United States. In relation to each country's GNP, U.S. direct production has eight times greater impact on the Japanese GNP than vice versa.

I am not trying to confuse anyone with these numbers but I want to see if these facts and figures agree with my readers' understanding and perspective. In formulating international strategies, if a businessperson formulates opinions and emotions like most scholars and journalists, who must appeal to the conventional wisdom and feelings of the public at large, then it is my fear that he or she will not be able to take advantage of objective—and often attractive—opportunities in critical overseas markets.

While American's historical and cultural links to Europe explain its investments there, the reasons for a perceived lack of ease and real participation on the part of the U.S. businesses in Japan probably stems from Japan's widely publicized regulatory restrictions and "unfair" competition. So let us examine the reality of these in terms of doing business in Japan.

Imposed Regulations

As one becomes an insider, one's complaints about the business environment decline. Or, one takes the environmental constraints for granted, and starts overcoming or going around them. Foreign corporations who are establishing a real insider position learn this process. Sometimes they can influence governmental policies much more strongly than domestic corporations.

For example, the pressure exerted by Motorola and other American companies on the Japanese government to open up Nippon Telephone and Telegraph's (NTT) procurement policy to competitors outside of the handful of manufacturers in the NTT family, has been tacitly applauded. This success will allow the thus far shut-out domestic companies to make participation bids to compete against traditional insiders like NEC and Fujitsu. Whether it will be more beneficial to the foreigners to fight against such competitive "new faces" as Matsushita, Canon, Sharp, and Sanyo is not clear. But these latter companies would certainly welcome the foreign pressure to open the heavy doors of NTT.

Another interesting use of foreign pressure by Japanese companies to deregulate traditional bureaucratic controls is seen in the area of financial institutions. The Ministry of Finance has exercised very tight controls, ranging from restrictions on outlet locations and business hours of banks to products and services rendered. The financial revolution around the world is making these forms of regulations meaningless. Almost every company is in consumer finance including, of course, banks and consumer credit unions. But the banks are under the Ministry of Finance, while the credit unions are under the MITI. Furthermore, postal savings—similar to banks' time deposit facilities—is under the Ministry of Posts and Telecommunications. Farmers' savings are under the auspices of Ministry of Fishery and Agriculture.

But everyone has started lending money to consumers in general. If a corporation wishes to be in consumer finance, it cannot afford to be governed and regulated by a "stoneheaded" ministry because competitive corporations might enjoy the unfair advantage of not being regulated by the same ministry. In such a situation, it is best for the insiders to stay quiet and let foreign financial institutions stir up the market to offset the traditional power balance between different Japanese ministries.

That's just what happened. The shockwaves caused in 1983 by Morgan Guaranty's application for a joint venture with Nomura Securities to set up a trust bank in Japan is best understood in such a light. Under Ministry of Finance guidance, security firms have not traditionally been allowed to enter into trust banking, which normally serves large pension funds and trust funds. Other U.S. banks are following suit by tying up with other major securities brokers like Yamaichi (which has affiliated with Chemical Bank and Bank of America). These delicate boundaries between different forms of financial institutions can only be understood by time-honored insiders, but they cannot reasonably be explained to a naive foreigner, particularly in this day and age of electronic banking.

Many regulations and guidelines have been removed in Japan over the past decade mainly through such subtle use of foreign pressure. For example, Citibank is now allowed to subscribe to long-term government bonds, a very prestigious position.

The governing agencies have also used these external pressures and demands because it is easier to explain the long-overdue changes to the outside parties. The net result of this "artificial" deregulation process is that Japan has very few remaining governmental hurdles. Many people still believe the image of Japanese markets of a decade or longer ago, when there were indeed lots of restrictions. Unless they take a fresh look, they are likely to fail to notice Japan as the rapidly liberalizing, second largest market in the Free World:

1. *Quotas* restricted some 490 product categories in Japan in the 1960s, virtually closing its domestic market to outsiders. Today, however, such quotas restrict only 27 product groups, of which 22 are agricultural and fishery commodities. Excluding agricultural categories, Japan has only 5 restricted product categories, fewer than America's 6, West Germany's 11, and France's 27.

The Japanese agricultural situation is worth mentioning. As I stated earlier, Japanese farmers, today totaling some 5 million, are not competitive in general. On the average, one farmer has only 1.1 hectares, or 2.7 acres. That is hardly larger than the land belonging to a suburban upper-middle-class house in the United States. The whole country is no larger than the state of California or Montana.

Less than 10 percent of Japan's land is arable, and the rest is mountainous. On this small piece of land, Japan had 15,764,000 farmers in 1950, just about 35 years ago. This number corresponds to 44.2 percent of the working population at that time. In 1960, the number had dropped to 13 million, or 29.8 percent of the total, and in 1970 it was 9.2 million or only 17.7 percent of the total working population.

Today, Japan's farming population is only 8.9 percent at 5 million, hardly a "majority" in terms of the total numbers of Japan's population. No modern government has been so successful at shifting its working population so dramatically from primary industries (agriculture, fisheries, and forestry) to secondary (industrial) and tertiary (service) industries in such a short time.

One of the reasons for Japan's industrial success lies in one key point arising from this shift in industrial spectrum: Japan's huge human reservoir of hardworking, masculine workers shifting from the farms with very low economic expectations in life. However, while shifting the country's work force, the Japanese government has made two rather critical concessions.

First, it decided to concentrate only on strategic crops, which means rice in the case of Japan. So today most of the rest of Japan's farm population cultivates rice, receiving government subsidies so that their income is roughly equivalent to that of typical urban workers. This means that Japanese rice costs roughly four times more than rice produced by the most competitive rice growers in the world, that is, California and Arkansas farmers. In fact, this government subsidy amounts to approximately $10 billion a year of taxpayers' money, and it represents one of the three biggest sources of governmental expenditures in Japan, along with health insurance and the national railway. In fact, with this kind of subsidy for rice, in two years Japan could purchase land in Arkansas equivalent to the total area occupied by all the rice paddies in Japan. Logically, then, the Japanese taxpayers would be completely free of such burdens.

A second concession has been made by the central government and also by the leading political party—the Liberal Democratic Party. That is, the Japanese voting system is not in direct proportion to population. In the crowded urban communities like Chiba and Kanagawa near Tokyo, the weight of one vote is only one sixth that of the vote of an individual in less-populated rural and farming districts, such as Shimane and Kagoshima. In other words, the distribution of the voting power is lagging behind changes in the distribution of the working population by at least 15 years. As a result, the farmers' group, which constitutes 8.9 percent of Japan's total population, can still exercise voting power greater than 18 percent. And because farmers are more united than urban workers and professionals (who are known as the "silent majority" and seldom vote), their relative influence can go up to 30 to 40 percent because the urban group's voting rate on average has been somewhat below 50 percent.

This is why Japanese farmers' political power has been overwhelmingly strong, and the government has had trouble removing the last remaining quotas on agricultural products. Mishandling this situation and pushing the remaining 5 million farmers further into a corner might force them to stop their traditional support of the conservative Liberal Democratic Party. As a result, the farmers might switch their allegiance to the Communist Party, which has become increasingly supportive of the farmers' protectionist sentiments.

Well-informed people are fully aware of this, but American journalists, politicians, and corporate executives have treated the subject too casually, thus making a solution extremely difficult.

2. *Tariffs* imposed on products in which U.S. producers have a competitive advantage are probably more irksome to Americans than Japan's quotas. Apart from citrus fruits, related agricultural products, and tobacco, tariffs cover 102 industrial items such as computers and related products,

plywood and veneer products, heavy electrical machinery, medical and diagnostic instruments, automotive tires, catalytic agents, steel, cosmetics, drugs, and televisions. Tariffs on these categories often price U.S. goods out of competition.

Substantial progress has been made recently to accelerate tariff reduction or eliminate tariffs altogether. In April and May 1982, as a result of a series of negotiations, these tariffs were reduced by some 35 percent on 1,635 items, with further reductions scheduled over the next five years. Overall, these reductions bring the average tariff rates on all industrial products (except oil) to 3.27 percent, a major reduction from 21 percent in 1960, 15 percent in 1970, and 4.3 percent in 1980. The 1982 figure of 3.27 percent compares favorably with those of the United States and the aggregate figures for the European Community, both estimated at 3.9 percent.

3. *Customs clearance procedures* are another source of frustration to American and European exporters. One complaint of Western exporters in the past has been the Japanese government's inconsistency. For example, U.S. customs officials issue a classification ruling based on a sample product and then the ruling is accepted by customs agents nationwide. Japanese customs officials, however, have made decisions on an individual basis, which has led to arbitrary rulings. The absence of practical uniform guidelines for customs clearance has also generated excessive paperwork.

In response to complaints, Japan's Ministry of Finance, together with other governmental ministries involved in customs procedures, adopted five measures aimed at simplifying customs examinations and reducing documentation requirements in April 1982.

In addition, earlier in 1982 the Japanese government established an Office of Trade Ombudsman to settle grievances related to the openness of the Japanese market, including import inspection procedures. While I am pretty sure that these measures would improve customs procedures, the crux of the issue has already become that of employment. A simplified customs system may mean unemployment for a few thousand officials in the Ministry of Justice as customs inspection would no longer require as much time. Since drugs and pistols are already tightly controlled in Japan and hence require very few inspecting officials, we cannot even redeploy laid-off officials in the criminal investigation sectors because for most offenses the arrest rate is already over 90 percent; there are simply few criminals left to catch. Similar to the situation in farming, here again we see that the risk of unemployment prevents the further implementation of a simplified customs system.

Structural and Cultural Differences

Probably the most perplexing hurdles for foreigners to Japan are those that reflect structural and cultural differences between the two nations. Nontariff barriers (NTBs) as perceived by foreigners to Japan range from differences in how standards are established to Japan's complex distribution system and distinct business practices and preferences.

One interesting psychological phenomenon I observe in discussions of NTBs is that few people see the other side of the coin: that difficulties of different kinds can exist and that the differences are usually not universal. If one gets used to a certain set of difficulties one starts to learn how to live with them, thereby taking them for granted. However, if the same person or company encounters a totally new set of difficulties it tends to treat these as "very difficult." Such difficulties can be labeled NTBs, especially in a foreign country. For example, a large American company is used to operating in a very complex sociopolitical environment of employment opportunities and antitrust laws. In Japan, such factors are not present, thereby making Japan a relatively free country in which to conduct business. However, foreign companies do not recognize this but instead tend to complain about different product approval processes and complex distribution systems. The Japanese companies, being so used to living with such difficulties as complex distribution systems, seldom label them NTBs; however, they certainly believe that operating in the United

States is a legal nightmare which they are not equipped to deal with. Hence, the U.S. legal complexities appear to Japanese corporations as America's NTBs. But now let us look at Japan's NTBs.

1. *Standards certification.* Japanese standards are said to be written often in a way that excludes foreign products from the Japanese market. The Japanese standards-setting process lacks easy understandability, making participation—and even access to information—by foreigners difficult. Other problems include nonacceptance of foreign test data, lack of approval for product ingredients generally recognized as safe worldwide, and the nontransferability of product approval.

America's food processing industry, for example, maintains that these standards are deliberately discriminatory. Unlike the United States and most other countries whose governments issue lists of additives generally accepted as safe for human consumption and a comparable list of substances banned, the Japanese have only one list. A specific additive can only be used for a specific purpose and only in a prescribed amount. Foods containing additives not on the so-called "positive" list may not be imported into Japan, even if those additives are not considered unsafe. The explicit policy of the Ministry of Health and Welfare is not to add additional ingredients to the positive list.

Regarded as an even more contentious problem is the fact that Japan does not accept the results of certain testing and certification procedures conducted outside Japan for certain products, such as drugs. The United States, on the other hand, generally accepts foreign data from testing done in accordance with appropriate U.S. standards and test procedures.

Furthermore, foreign manufacturers cannot apply directly to Japanese ministries for product approval. Only an approved Japanese entity can hold approval rights. Until recently, if foreign exporters wanted to change agents, their new agents had to reapply for product approval unless their formerly "approved" agents were willing to give up their rights. Of course, American firms could circumvent this constraint by establishing a subsidiary in Japan—but this option is not necessarily open to all manufacturers.

Needless to say, these measures are not necessarily de-signed to block out foreign companies. Rather, they are reflec-tive of the traditional Japanese value system based on "relationship," as opposed to paper-based contracts.

The Japanese ministries usually rely on various industry associations when framing a specific standard or regulation. Again, this is reflective of their consensus-seeking approach. However, those associations usually are made up of the larger, well-established organizations. Although a recent survey by the American Chamber of Commerce in Japan showed that, of the U.S. firms who responded, the majority of those applying for membership were admitted, it also indicated that Ameri-can firms were ambivalent about the value of membership. Fewer than half felt it was in their firm's interest to join. Some were reluctant due to antitrust considerations, and oth-ers felt association membership was best evaluated on a case-by-case basis. Obviously, mastery of the Japanese language would be one major prerequisite for getting any real value out of membership in an association.

A further handicap to foreigners is that Japanese standards are often set to design rather than performance specifications. This is perceived by the U.S. government to be in direct con-travention of Japan's obligations under the Standards Code of the General Agreement on Tariffs and Trade and under the 1979 United States–Japan Joint Statement in Standards, Testing, and Certification Procedures.

On the positive side, however, is the fact that Japan is a single country, and there is usually only one standard to satisfy, the Japan Industrial Standard. One of my first assignments as a consultant was to assist a Japanese pipe manufacturer to figure out how to enter into the U.S. market.

The more we studied the situation, the less optimistic we became. For, in order for this innovative pipe to be used, it had to be approved and listed by each municipality, irriga-tion district, and water district. In other words, this company had to be prepared to visit one corps of engineers and one laboratory after another, across the entire United States. Of course, we selected several high-priority districts in order to get a beachhead in the vast U.S. landmass. Both my consulting firm and this company felt this was the way to do business in the United States, and did not complain about the "nontariff barrier" which had been making the long-established incumbent companies much more privileged competitors.

These differences have historical origins and are very difficult to circumvent. For companies established as insiders, the barriers seldom become an annoyance. But to those companies at the doorstep these hurdles may appear as major barriers to entry. Successful multinationals have conquered all of these structural hurdles by becoming an insider in each key market.

2. *Distribution system.* One of the most frequently stated hindrances is the way products reach the ultimate user. It is true that the Japanese distribution system, which has evolved over the past three centuries, is one of the most perplexing in the world. In Japan, as elsewhere, the distribution of goods from producers to retailers generally involves wholesalers. A rough estimate published by Japan's Manufactured Imports Promotion Organization shows that, until recently, the ratio of wholesale to direct sales was 4:1 in Japan as compared to 1.9:1 in Great Britain, 1.7:1 in West Germany, 1.6:1 in the United States, and 1.2:1 in France.

The multilayered wholesale process, involving two or more go-betweens, is largely a financing and logistics operation in disguise, one in which large wholesalers give smaller wholesalers—who can offer "personalized" services to smaller manufacturers—longer payment terms.

At the other end of the distribution system, wholesalers allow de facto consignment sales by accepting return of unsold goods and by vastly extending the range of manufactured goods a small retailer can offer. Even in highly concentrated industries, heavy participation by wholesalers can be extremely effective if the product carries a low unit price or is in high demand as a daily necessity (such as cosmetics, film, synthetic detergents, processed foods, etc.) so that retailers are able to carry a fairly diverse stock. In other words, in the United States the retailers must have economies-of-scale since they have to master the art of selling a rich assortment of products. In Japan, small retailers can survive because most of the assortment function is done by the wholesalers.

In recent years, the many-layered distribution system, especially in the consumer goods area, has come under attack. Shaklee, for example, surprised Japanese drug distributors by directly transferring their successful recipe of door-to-door sales directly from the United States. According to a Japanese Ministry of Health and Welfare ordinance, drugs must be sold at a fixed location where there is one pharmacist and measuring equipment to prepare medicine according to prescription. Vitamin pills, long classed as drugs, had been sold through over-the-counter channels for this reason although this had not been consciously recognized. However, vitamins and other nutrition pills are actually foods and not drugs. So there is nothing wrong in selling these pills directly to the consumer. Japanese pharmaceutical companies, watching Shaklee's phenomenal takeoff, could not move. They were afraid of harming relationships with the traditional middlemen, namely wholesalers and over-the-counter retailers on whom they still had to rely for distribution of ethical and over-the-counter drugs.

In recent years, a lot has been said about the complex Japanese distribution system. Some criticize it as Japan's NTB against foreign imports, and others call it part of the cultural heritage of inefficiency. However, there is nothing cast in concrete about it, or no law written not to change it. In fact, if you observe what is happening in the Japanese distribution system at the microscopic level, you would have to conclude that major structural changes are in progress, already creating (or depolarizing) the winners and the losers.

Chainstores

In the consumer retail area, supermarkets made deep inroads during the mid-1960s into the arena of the then dominant stores and mom-and-pop shops. These new chainstores now account for 40 percent of total consumer goods distribution, and some winners (for example, Daiei, Seibu, Nichii, JUSCO, Ito-Yokado, Marui) have all become multi-billion-dollar national networks. Founder–CEOs of these chainstores are still in their fifties and their companies are run in a dynamic, entrepreneurial fashion.

Fifteen years ago, it was considered good manners to respect—and even fear—the power of the big department stores, and not to talk about acquiring them. Now, Isao Nakauchi of Daiei and Takuya Okada of JUSCO, for example, laugh at such do's and don'ts in retailing, since they have not accepted the traditional notion of good corporate manners. To demonstrate this, Nakauchi even tried to take over the prestigious Takashimaya Department Store. Also, most supermarkets have grown by aggressively combining new start-up and acquisition strategies, except for Ito-Yokado.

These supermarket entrepreneurs have now diversified into fast food stores, family restaurants, convenience stores, and other retail chain operations, mostly by tying up with successful U.S. franchise operators. The affiliations of Seven-Eleven and Denny's with Masatoshi Ito's Ito-Yokado are probably the most successful among the dozens of such tie-ups. The net effect of them all has been to accelerate the decline of small-scale retailers while converting many potential losers to franchise operators of winning chains.

Given the high degree of success of American-style chain operations, it seems that there has been no practical barrier to entry. Rather, the critical factor was in choosing the Japanese partner. Where established big names are chosen as a partner, results have not been good. For example, Dunkin' Donuts tied up with Seibu but could not grow beyond 50 stores. Meanwhile, Mister Donut allied with Duskin and has 410 stores. The latter is clearly the winner in Japan. The success of Mister Donut can be attributed to a young man named Koji Chiba, who has singlehandedly pioneered the market for donuts, a totally new snack concept for the Japanese only a decade ago.

Den Fujita of McDonald's is another tycoon whose entrepreneurial and venturesome business mind has pushed this American-born hamburger chain to the no. 2 position in the fast food industry, at $362 million in annual turnover with 395 outlets.

The supermarkets, having moved into restaurants and other retail chains, are now moving to form "buying groups," similar to what has become a major purchasing power in West Germany. For example, CGC, led by Daiei, has 15 billion dollars worth of bargaining power, when its 150 group companies are added together. Likewise, JUSCO, UNI, Izumiya, and Chujitsuya have joined hands to form a similar buying group, named Aiku, to counter Daiei's move, at the same time exerting strong pressure on manufacturers to lower wholesale prices. So much so that the Japanese Fair Trade Commission has announced that it has a "keen interest" in observing this volume discount practice.

Discounters

The second half of the 1970s was an important period for Japanese retail distribution. Unlike department stores and supermarkets, which carry a full range of consumer goods, there has been a surge of specialized discounters. These discounters attacked mainly the consumer durables characterized by high unit price, low frequency of purchase, and high distribution margin. Currently, a wide spectrum of markets have been hard hit by the discounters, including home appliances, brown goods (televisions and stereos), cameras, glasses, jewelry, sporting goods, men's suits, tires, and do-it-yourself tools. Most of these discounters sell well-established national brands at 25 to 30 percent below the manufacturer's suggested retail price. And these discounters get their merchandise from all over the world as long as the goods are of high quality and the deals are acceptable—of course, on the discounters' terms!

Discounters, like their U.S. equivalent (for example, 47th Street Photo in New York City), advertise heavily but carry narrower model selections with much higher turnover than regular specialized stores. They are typically run by an individual who is bold and creative, and who is determined to challenge the status quo of the established network. For example, the one store of Akikazu Fujisawa's Yodobashi Camera is responsible for as much as 30 percent of the total single-lens reflex camera sales in the Tokyo Metropolitan area. Manufacturers, fearful of alienating captive wholesalers and traditional mom-and-pop camera shops, tried not to sell to Yodobashi. Only a few years ago, many manufacturers even gave their employees cash and sent them to Yodobashi's shop in Shinjuku to buy up stocks of their company's cameras so that Yodobashi would at least be out of stock of their products.

However, today most manufacturers cannot ignore Yodobashi, because low store sales there would hurt their share of the national market. As a result, camera manufacturers even send "helpers" to promote sales of their own brand in Yodobashi shops. A small sign at the entrance of Yodobashi's main shop in Shinjuku, which reads "Wholesalers, please go directly to the office upstairs," signifies Yodobashi's victory. Today, Yodobashi's bargaining power against the camera manufacturers is such that it is cheaper for a middleman to buy from Yodobashi than directly from manufacturers under formal contracts.

Likewise, Shigeru Morino's Megane Drug Company distributes prestigious brands of eyeglasses such as Rodenstock and Metzler and sells them at 50 percent discount compared with traditional outlets. Nobody before Morino's time capitalized on the built-in vulnerability of the industry, in which distribution was responsible for 70 percent of the list price. The high margin of distribution is mainly because eyeglasses go through three stages of distribution, and because outlets tend to stockpile inventory to suit all kinds of customer tastes and prescriptions.

Similar surprise attacks have been successfully launched by Akira Watanabe of Shintomi Gorufu in golf goods, Yoshitake Ogino of Winter Victoria in ski and ski-related fashion wear, Kazuomi Kimura of Miki in jewelry, Toshio Sumino of Autobacks in tire and car accessories, and Takanori Matsumoto of JACS in used car sales. Several similar attempts are being made in the areas of fishing equipment, tennis goods, furniture, and even personal computers. One interesting variation is Reikodo in music record rental. Kiyokazu Ohura challenged the rigid and well-protected record distribution industry, and started a rental shop charging only 50 cents for membership, and another 50 cents for an overnight rental. While it has been much criticized and there are lawsuits against it, Reikodo has grown to 150 outlets, with $20 million in annual turnover within two years.

Perhaps a more fundamental and far reaching change is in the home appliance and brown goods distribution area. This is one area where the Big Three (Matsushita, Toshiba, and Hitachi) have built, over the past 20 years, an awesome 75,000 franchised (mom-and-pop) appliance outlets for both white and brown goods. However, these outlets follow close guidelines regarding resale prices and restrictions on selling competitor's brands, in exchange for financial and operational assistance from their franchisers. Their challengers, Best Denki (Mitsuo Kitada), Daiichi Katei Denki, Ishimaru, Yamagiwa, Nisshin, and Laox, mushroomed in the 1970s by offering prices 25 to 30 percent lower than the franchised mom-and-pop stores.

These chainstores, known as Kaden Ryohanten—for home appliance mass merchandiser—now account for 20 percent of the $20 billion white and brown goods markets in Japan. Manufacturers, having found that their traditional strengths with a large number of captive outlets can become serious weaknesses, initially tried to contain Ryohanten. But today they can no longer ignore them because some of them are so well managed and big (for example, Best Denki sales totaled 73.1 billion yen during 1983 with 259 outlets), and the traditional mom-and-pop store's future does not look so bright.

Most first-generation franchised home appliance store owners are past their mid-fifties and the problem of succession to ownership is everywhere. Companies like Matsushita even have special training schools to discipline the "spoiled" second generation.

Meanwhile, brown goods, especially stereo components, have become so sophisticated that not all mom-and-pop stores are up to date with the audio buffs. The audio experts among consumers now go to the Ryohantens, such as Laox and Ishimaru, because the store clerks in these stores are much more specialized and well versed. So the Ryohantens today have not only discount prices but also offer product knowledge to sell high-class consumer electronics, including personal computers.

The net result is a decay of the time-honored and complex distribution systems and the emergence of rather sophisticated mass merchandisers for home audio, video, and information systems.

These discounters are not free of trouble. A typical pattern is for the prime-mover founder-owner to forget about the fundamentals of discounting: cash purchases and sales, high turnover of limited product lines, and low personnel and shop costs. As the founder-owners get rich, they start decorating their shops, paying more to employees, dealing with low turnover but prestigious luxury lines, and accepting credit sales.

Ryutsu-Oroshiuri-Centre (ROC) once revolutionized the men's ready-made suit market by bypassing wholesalers and offering suits at 26,900 yen, or one-half the price of equivalent suits in traditional outlets. However, its founder, Isamune Kinoshita, tried to expand the number of outlets too rapidly, and diversified into a high-risk, high-return fish farming venture. He found himself out of cash in less than five years into his glorious challenge. What he has left behind is ROC's price tag: now one can get men's suits at (or even below) 26,900 yen, everywhere.

ROC is not alone in this venturesome game. Matsunami in home appliances, Aiworld in sundry goods, and Peti Road in jewelry have all challenged existing distribution and gone belly up before their mission was over.

Manufacturer's Challenge

While discount outlets have been the attempts of middlemen or retailers to vertically integrate the intermediate steps in distribution, manufacturers have not sat still and watched the show.

Kao Soap, Japan's no. 1 toiletry goods manufacturer, has spent over ten years building up the *hansha* (the company controlled regional distributors) in lieu of traditional wholesale outlets in the toiletry industry. This *hansha* format is probably most frequently used when bypassing one step in distribution, and typically invites local capital (or exwholesaler) participation. Since labor conditions and wage levels regarding local wholesalers when compared to prestigious manufacturers are significantly different (that is, labor conditions and wage levels at manufacturers are much higher), these vertical integrations take at least five to ten years to implement. Moving too hastily makes the *hansha* an expensive but ineffective channel, because wholesalers, still enjoying lower-cost labor and better economies-of-scale, can sabotage the sales of the products of the manufacturer intending to form a *hansha*. Wholesalers, while their long-term viability and controllability are questionable, are a convenient channel for making quick sales. The transition to the *hansha* requires a decade-long, nerve-racking maneuver involving gradually shifting seven basic distribution functions (sales, advertising, finance, inventory, service, physical distribution, and customer/competitor information collection) to the manufacturer's own sales organization.

As such, institutionally run big establishments have great difficulty in executing such a move because their executive tenure in any given function is typically two to six years, and their planning horizon, unfortunately, is three to five years. As a result, the big establishments tend to develop a detailed distribution plan using existing channels. That is why bold moves to bust established modus operandi in distribution frequently come from relatively small, entrepreneur-run companies.

Makita in power tools, Mori in numerical control (NC) machines, Daio in paper, and Gakushu Kenkyusha in book publishing have all gone "direct" successfully. Makita, for example, has cleverly taken over from distributors such critical functions as sales and service. When distributors recognized this subtle change, Makita's own sales force was much closer to where the action was with professional power tool users, like carpenters and plumbers. Makita, instead of terminating

99

its distributors altogether, gave them only the *choai* (collecting money) function. Today, Makita has captured 40 percent of Japan's power tool market and is highly respected for its no-debt financial position.

Had other establishments like Hitachi Koki and Shinko moved in unison, Makita would not have been able to reap the profits, which was one of the natural consequences of its bold move.

In the industrial goods area, most companies are also trying to go direct. But here the choice seems to be severely influenced by the users. Many of them prefer to use distributors because of product range and selection, installation and servicing, less-stringent payment terms, and total systems know-how which are not restricted to the particular machine in question. Manufacturers are now setting up engineering and installation subsidiaries to establish these functions on their own. However, most of them lack suitable personnel, and many such subsidiaries have become convenient dumping grounds for senior managers before their normal retirement age, which is from 57 to 60, is reached. As a result, these newly formed subsidiaries must rely on traditional distributors and, hence, they are adding one or two extra layers to the already complex sales and marketing activities.

In the public sector businesses (water treatment, civil construction, housing, and railway), distributors have a rather positive role, the most important of which is to maintain "relationships" with the bureaucrats and decision-influencing politicians. Here, prestigious manufacturers do not want to get involved in such unofficial activities, so they use distributors that are willing to do a "good job" within a token margin. Such a practice is under strong public scrutiny today, and may, in fact, disappear before long. That will trigger a major move by manufacturers in this sector to really go direct.

All in all, the Japanese distribution system is in turmoil and changing. Nothing is cast in concrete and is culturally fixed. In fact, McKinsey works with several large Japanese companies that are changing the structure of distribution in a major way. Once you become an insider, and analyze forces at work, there is not a single element that you cannot change. Establishments, big distributors, government agencies, and even customers will discourage bold moves at times. But in the long run, when you are determined to challenge the status quo which is not based on economic principles and hence not in the long-term interest of anybody, there are certainly attractive opportunities to create a Nakauchi or a Fujisawa.

To those foreign companies and governments that complain about the complexities of the Japanese distribution system, the aforementioned business heroes and heroes-to-be would say, "Come on and join us. Let's have fun together busting the system!"

3. *Preference and peculiarities.* The Japanese are probably among the most demanding consumers in the Free World today. In the course of four decades, they have grown from a war-devastated economy with few goods except imports from which to choose, to the second richest capitalist economy with a diverse selection of goods. Goods no longer sell just because they are foreign.

Another cause of frustration among foreign firms is the totally different value system that governs the way business is conducted in Japan. Business relationships frequently are measured in length of time. Negotiations are conducted without legal contracts and are based on human relationships. Agreements are "modifiable" as circumstances change because the Japanese value long-term associations with clients rather than short-term exploitation. Discriminatory rebates are acceptable as signs of good will. All of these practices make doing business in Japan different and demanding—but hardly "protected" or prohibitive.

Although, as noted earlier, this is very much the age of the universal product, where "ABBA, Levi's, and McDonald's" know no national boundaries, the Japanese do have distinct tastes. Yet, American merchandisers push such products as oversize cars with left-wheel drive, devices measuring in inches, appliances not adapted to lower voltage and frequencies, office equipment without *kanji* capabilities and clothes not cut to smaller dimensions. Most Japanese like sweet or-

101

anges and sour cherries, not vice versa. That is because they compare imported oranges with domestic *mikans* (very sweet tangerines) and cherries with domestic plums (somewhat tangy and sour).

A very good recent example is the Barbie doll. This American best-seller did not do very well for a long time. And its creator, Mattel Toys International, gave the manufacturing license to Takara, a Japanese doll and toy specialist. Takara's own survey revealed that most Japanese girls—and their parents—thought the doll's breasts were too big and the legs unrealistically long. After making these minor modifications (Exhibit 8–1), and converting the Barbie dolls blue eyes to dark brown, Takara started selling the same doll under the same brand name and concept, only to find out this time that its production could not catch up with the demand. Takara sold some two million Barbie dolls in just two years. Takara's planning manager, Shusuke Kubota, says, "Dolls in Japan are reflection of what girls want to be. With the target customer group in Japan being eighth-graders, this doll had to look more polished and fashionable than the original version. What sells in the United States does not necessarily sell in Japan. But the [sound] concept can be transferred with intelligent interpretation and translation."

"Another example," says Koji Chiba of Mister Donut, "is the use of cinnamon. When we first introduced donuts in Japan, our consumer tests indicated that most Japanese did not care for cinnamon. So I thought I'd reduce the content dramatically at first. But what is a donut without cinnamon? Over the next five to six years, we have gradually increased our donuts' cinnamon content at a pace our customers could get used to. Today, our donuts contain the same amount of cinnamon as in the United States. It has taken a long time, but as far as the taste buds are concerned, we have converted the Japanese into liking cinnamon over the past decade."

Mister Donut's success is the result of a series of such minute, but sensible, modifications. Their coffee cup is smaller and lighter, to fit the finger size of the average Japanese consumer. Even their donuts are a little smaller than those in the United States.

by Takara
(Japan)

by Mattel
(United States)

EXHIBIT 8-1   Barbie doll.

A similar experience is reported with McDonald's hamburgers. The Japanese like ground beef mixed with fat and minced onions. That is the concept of the Japanese hamburger. So when McDonald's first came to Japan, they had to adjust the red meat content. In the United States, even dogs like pure meat, as in the Alpo commercial! But that was not so in Japan. But, over the past decade, most hamburger chains have succeeded in bringing up the red meat content, and today it is almost the same as in the United States.

Japanese Scotch whiskey is not made in Scotland, but

rather by Suntory in Japan. It has 78 percent share of the $3.6 billion market. Because most Japanese prefer to drink *mizuwari,* or whisky diluted with five to ten times the amount of water, most good Scotch whiskeys do not taste good at that level of dilution. Suntory tastes much better when diluted. Its most successful product, *daruma,* or Black Bottle, tastes like Johnnie Walker (Red Label). Many companies tried to promote "real" Scotch to no avail, until they learned the trade secret and developed their blends accordingly.

Likewise, brandy was initially a rather special liquor which did not have much success in Japan. Suntory, again using the tactic of diluting it with five to ten times the amount of water and ice, called the drink an "American." They used Cheryl Ladd's "all-American girl" image in their television commercials. And Suntory brandy became a phenomenally popular drink for sophisticated ladies. Because the Japanese are brought up drinking mild alcoholic beverages such as beer and sake, they like to dilute alcohol by a factor of 10 to 13 when it is served, regardless of the particular blend's specific origin, be it a malt or distillation process.

These are minor changes in the main concept. They can be compared to an "ad lib" or improvisation on a musical theme. Sensitivity, or preparedness, to these ad libs is crucial when foreign firms conduct business in Japan or other overseas nations. In most cases, if the basic concept of product and service and the supporting business infrastructure are sound, there is better than a 50–50 chance of success, so long as the new competitor has ears to hear and eyes to see the local tastes.

Tokyo's Disneyland attracted some 10 million visitors in its first year of operation, raking in 300 million dollars. Walt Disney Productions gets 10 percent of the admission fees, and 5 percent of the receipts on food and souvenirs. That is not bad for a relatively risk-free export of accumulated know-how. But this phenomenal success has been possible because Walt Disney Productions had a sound concept which the Japanese people, with their universally trained tastes, would accept. Disney was also able to pull together a group of willing investors for the $650 million project, such as Keisei, Mitsui, Fuji Film, and Matsushita. Once one becomes an insider, things no longer look "strange" even for a *gaijin* (foreigner).

What works in the West works in Japan, and vice versa. The critical point of departure is the amount of modification. But before one goes ahead with major modifications, let us look at the internal inhibitors that have blurred the eyes and ears of U.S. and European corporations in order to see what's really required to be successful in Japan.

Internal Inhibitors

Apart from failing to recognize and deal with the special needs and conditions of the Japanese market or to modify products to cater to customer preferences, some corporations have internal inhibitors preventing their success in Japan, or for that matter, in any foreign country. The primary inhibitor is management's mentality.

The firm's financial expectations, in many cases, may be inappropriate for Japan. Most American executives measure performance on the basis of return on investment and ROA, which are usually considerably higher than what Japanese competitors require. Broadly, the rate of return on total assets and sales for U.S. companies is about two times greater than that for Japanese corporations. Return on sales, not investment, is the yardstick by which most Japanese industrial companies measure their successes. This concern with return on sales is the rule, particularly among diverse, multiproduct organizations. To be more specific, many Japanese companies would be quite content with increased sales and operating margins, even if the ratio between the two (that is, return on sales) were declining. Their decision to invest in a product or business are seldom made on the basis of a quantified profits projection or a detailed timetable of eventual payoff.

When this generally lower return and its implicit marketing focus to gain the necessary share is coupled with an extended payback time, investment in Japan can seem unattractive. For example, even a minimal level of upfront investment in Japan requires a payback period of three years.

In addition, to set up a small office, say 780 sq. ft. in Tokyo, would run from $150,000 to $250,000 for the first year. This estimate includes rent advances and deposits (again a unique Japanese system of "key money"), redecorating, furniture, and one bilingual secretary. This does not even include management salaries or expenses. The initial cost of establishing a larger office, say 7,100 sq. ft., again exclusive of management salaries, runs about $1 million to $1.5 million for the first year in central Tokyo. The cost of establishing an office in Osaka is about 60 percent of the amount for Tokyo. By implication, the payout period for any sort of manufacturing operation requiring a sizable site would be considerably longer.

In part a cause and in part a symptom of still another hurdle to be faced by a firm's headquarters is how a firm locates Japan within the corporate scheme of things. Corporations tend to view their corporate headquarters as the center of the world. Few firms think in terms of the size or strategic importance of Japan. Few organizational hierarchies reflect its potential or its profit contribution. Even among sophisticated multinationals with highly profitable operations in Japan, the country is viewed as an extension of the export or overseas sales department and frequently is on an organizational par with a branch office in Hong Kong.

Despite Japan's economic prowess and strategic importance, it is often regarded as another, albeit problem-prone, Asian sales region. In many segments, Japan's potential approximates half that of the total U.S. market. Yet, many multinationals deploy resources to Japan that are less than those deployed to California, and often less than those destined for New Jersey or Connecticut.

Most corporations lump Japan together with Korea, Taiwan, and Hong Kong and call it all the Far East. Others put Japan with the members of the Association of Southeast Asian Nations (ASEAN), and classify it in Asia. A fashionable treatment of Japan in recent years is to put it with ASEAN, Australia, and Chile and call the whole group the "Pacific Basin." If organization follows strategy, as Alfred Chandler says, then this kind of classification must implicitly assume that competitive moves and customer desires, namely, the two critical elements of strategy, in Japan are identical to those of ASEAN member countries and Chile. No wonder these companies are outmaneuvered easily by the powerful competitors and even by local imitators. They are simply not organized to win in Japan, let alone to become a true insider and establish resilient staying power in times of turbulence.

Interestingly, this perceptual gap at headquarters is often exacerbated by a resident home office expert, whose first-hand exposure to Japan is out of date or limited to a short fact-finding jaunt once a year. Overall, many local managers regard headquarters' misperceptions as the single biggest barrier to success in Japan.

During our study for the United States–Japan TSG, we conducted extensive field interviews with expatriate executives who headed their Japanese subsidiaries. They were the generals who were fighting the war on the "most difficult" front. Interestingly, very few of them cited the popular theories of NTBs and regulations as the hindrance. Rather, they were almost unanimously troubled by their headquarters' attitudes. Listen to these voices directly:

> Most people at home don't understand the Japanese business attitude, where the prime responsibility is to employees.
>
> (A chemical company executive)

> Headquarters people think they understand, but they don't.
>
> (A diversified conglomerate manager)

> Head office now understands that it does not understand Japan.
>
> (A consumer products company executive)

> The "not invented here" syndrome exists in the U.S.
>
> (An office products company manager)

> [My company] did not understand the Japanese market at time of entry and still does not understand it adequately.
>
> (A chemical company local president)

> Given a fresh start, [my firm] would have less of a short-term profit orientation and would market more aggressively.
>
> (A food company president)

107

Home office criteria are sales and profit growth; Japanese criteria are market share versus other foreign companies.

(A cosmetic company executive)

[We] get all the head office attention we need. If given a fresh start, we'd listen more and earlier to our Japanese partners.

(An office equipment company executive)

[Head office] did not try to understand the Japanese market but adopted a missionary/colonial attitude.

(A consumer products company local president)

It is not uncommon for a ready-to-retire executive to head up operations in Japan. Seldom is this individual's exposure and experience recycled back into corporate headquarters. In many cases, a person recently returned from Japan is relocated to some other division that has nothing to do with Japan.

Perception Gap

Despite the pitfalls, penalties, and red tape, many foreign firms have made it in Japan. Coca-Cola is no. 1 in the Japanese soft drinks market. Nestle has been in Japan for almost 40 years, and dominates the market with a 70 percent share in instant coffee. IBM employed nearly 15,000 people in Japan alone in 1983. These are all 100 percent owned subsidiaries.

The American and European perception of Japan is that Japan concentrates its industry development with the clear intention of destroying Western industries one after another. This is the so-called "Japan conspiracy" fable. The Japanese, on the other hand, think that the Germans have the clear intention of destroying the Japanese chemical industry, through the massive R&D and cost competitiveness of BASF, Bayer, and Hoechst.

And the Americans have, the Japanese say, the clear intention of corrupting the Japanese with their fast food. If one looks at the unprecedented speed of change in dietary habit of a nation as big as 120 million in population, one might be led to believe in the "American conspiracy" theory. These include those numerous outlets of the chain operators that did not exist at all in the 1960s in Japan: McDonald's, Kentucky Fried Chicken, Wimpy, Mister Donut, Baskin-Robbins, Shakey's, Denny's, and Seven-Eleven, just to mention a few conspicuous other fast food chains one notices as one walks the streets of Tokyo. Even such recent phenomenon as David's Cookies and Mrs. Field's have made entries into Japan.

These fast food outlets often carry Del Monte ketchup, Coca-Cola, Seven-Up, and Tetrapak milk. Supermarkets usually carry Scottie and Kleenex tissues, Lux soap and Woolite detergent, Staedtler rubber erasers, V-8 juice, Knorr, Campbell and Maggi soups, Nestle coffee and Lipton tea, McCormick spices, Ritz crackers, Kellogg's corn flakes, Granola bars, Kodak film, Dannon yogurt, and Borden cheese.

Drugstores are full of American and European brands—Nivea skin cream, Max Factor and Revlon cosmetics, Herb candy, Vicks cough drops, Contac capsules, and Bayer aspirin, just to name a few. On the more prestigious side (and still very popular and successful) in Japan are Cross, Shaeffer, and Parker pens, Louis Vuitton, Givenchy, and Nina Ricci bags, Yves Saint Laurent, Pierre Cardin, and Ungaro fashions, and Estee Lauder, Clinique, and Chanel cosmetics.

All of the brand name sporting goods flood Japanese tennis courts, golf courses, and ski slopes, ranging from Adidas, Lacoste, Teng, and Fila to Wilson, Blizzard, Kneissl, Prince, and Head. In fact, these brands know no national boundaries. Sure, many of these brands are licensed, but licensing was the strategic choice of these branded goods producers. Whether or not the concept would be carried out on their own or by others through licensing was a separate matter.

The point is that when it comes to purchasing decisions, the Japanese consumers, like any other Triadians or OECD-ites, do not really care where the goods come from. They like what others like, or they like what they like.

Keys to Success

"Making it" in Japan is more than a matter of accepting the regulatory requirements and adjusting to indigenous procedures and protocol. Successful entry demands having a strong "plus" to bring to the market. Survival, in turn, takes a strong degree of commitment, creativity, and competitiveness—the three Cs. When a joint venture or joint working arrangement is involved, selection of the right partner is often critical. The partner's size can be a critical criterion (whether too big to control or coordinate, or too small to be effective) and should be evaluated carefully.

Japan itself is a sophisticated market with a highly developed economy. Its R&D expenditures are high, much of its technology is advancing quickly both in performance and market value, and its production methods are emulated worldwide. In addition, Japan is a very unforgiving economy, destroying some 19,000 corporations annually through bankruptcy, and these losers rarely get a second chance.

And yet, there are many winners and winning brands of foreign origin. What distinguishes the leaders from the poor performers? What can be learned from this comparison? It is this focus, so fundamental to success in the domestic environment, but even more so overseas, that we need to consider.

Obviously, a firm must bring an added value into a foreign milieu. Our TSG findings show that winners appear to share one or more of four basic prerequisites when they *entered* the market: (1) a resource-driven product, because Japan is not strong in resource-based industries; (2) a technological lead; (3) a "new-to-Japan" concept; and (4) a differentiated marketing strategy. If one does not have any of these "antes," then one should realize that one is in a "me-too" game in an unforgiving foreign territory.

However, even with these leads, success does not follow automatically. For foreigners, overcoming the structural and cultural constraints inherent in an alien environment and staying well ahead of the challenge of Japan's inimitable imitators takes a sustained effort. In other words, the "antes" are not good enough conditions for success in an ongoing phase.

Staying power is something else. Although bringing a resource advantage to a nation that has few of nature's bounties upon which to draw may give a firm a definite edge, all other advantages must be assiduously protected against competitive thrusts. This requires constant attention, especially considering the fact that even a technological lead no longer assures a sustainable edge for long. A firm must consistently upgrade and modify its product and/or service offering in order to maintain the edge against hard-working competitors.

The real success factors, or the three Cs, reflect this point. In short, it is staying power as an insider that is required for real success during the ongoing phase of an overseas operation. Let us examine these three Cs.

Success Factor No. 1—Commitment

Probably the single most critical success factor for successful overseas operations is commitment—in time, money, and effort. It comes as no real surprise to learn that foreign firms with long-term success in Japan have made a significant commitment. They have adjusted their short-term return success expectations accordingly, and have bridged—in various ways and to varying degrees—the delicate human relations problems that arise from differences in customs and culture.

The selection, development, and retention of local personnel is one expression of commitment. Successful foreign-affiliated companies share certain characteristics. They tend to:

△ Emulate the hiring practice of leading Japanese firms that select new college graduates and train internally

△ Keep the personnel turnover rate low to build employee identification with firm goals (foreign-affiliated companies are not always perceived to be a permanent part of the scene)

△ Invest both time and money in the development of skills among local staff.

Although investment requirements can vary and the effort expended is measured in relative terms, one universal

111

gauge of commitment is time. Patience is one expression of time commitment. A five-year wait for profits must become acceptable, if one thinks of establishing a new company afresh. However, when it comes to entering a new overseas market, most corporations use financial criteria typically developed for domestic diversification and/or expansion into countries with a similar cultural heritage. Successful U.S. and European companies in Japan typically plan in terms of decades instead of years, particularly when it comes to human resources development.

Success Factor No. 2—Creativity

Creativity is a subjective measure and a difficult one to judge looking at success after the fact. How much of a company's success is due to happenstance, and how much to strategic maneuvering? Be that as it may, the ability to look at obstacles as a creative challenge is certainly another characteristic shared by most winners.

Wella's case is a familiar example of a creative approach to the Japanese market. Instead of competing head-on with the Japanese giant manufacturers in the traditional supermarket outlets where shampoo is sold alongside soap and toothpaste, Wella designed its product as a beauty aid to be sold with cosmetics and other high-end personal care items. As a result, Wella was able to introduce its products in several untraditional outlets—drug and cosmetics stores as well as beauty parlors and barbers. Today, Wella products can be seen virtually everywhere shampoo is sold—including neighborhood supermarkets.

There are other creative stories: one major chemical company tailored the flow behavior of engineering plastics to meet Japanese design criteria. McDonald's shunned suburban outlets—so successful for this firm in the United States—to concentrate on capturing the flow of commuter traffic in the heart of central Tokyo and other major cities. Warner Lambert used the nationwide distribution channel of a cutlery wholesaler to distribute its Schick ejector razor and succeeded in changing the shaving habits of the nation—from evening in *ofuro* (bath) to the morning with their spray foam.

Success Factor No. 3—Competitiveness

Although competitiveness stems, in a large part, from a firm's commitment and its strategic creativity, it can be an important factor on its own. Competitiveness often reflects the firm's willingness to take the plunge ahead of market leaders. Often, the number one firm in the United States does not necessarily achieve the premier position in Japan. For example, Schick is bigger in Japan than Gillette, and Mister Donut has ten times more outlets than Dunkin' Donuts in Japan.

Omark Industries has carved out a dominant niche in the Japanese chainsaw replacement market. It entered Japan over 30 years ago—in 1951, some 14 years before other foreign competitors—using Japan's traditional distribution system.

Max Factor paved the way in Japan some 20 years before any other foreign cosmetic maker. Although viewed as a popular-priced product in the United States, Max Factor has maintained its image among Japan's cosmopolitan set as a quality product. The fact that it develops half of its products in Japan and tailors 30 percent of all others to fit the tastes of its Japanese users has contributed significantly to their success to date.

Interestingly, this same push to be competitive is observed among Japanese companies going abroad. A small supermarket chain called Yaohan in Shizuoka Prefecture failed to become a retailer of national scale in Japan in competition against such giants as Daiei and Ito-Yokado. However, Yaohan opened its first store in Singapore in 1974, and now is the largest retailer there with six full-scale stores.

Likewise, nobody knows in Japan what Fujitec is. It is actually the smallest elevator manufacturer among such firms as Mitsubishi, Hitachi, Toshiba, and Toyo Otis (owned by Matsushita). However, Fujitec has found customers throughout Southeast Asia and the United States. In 1983, the company moved its headquarters from Tokyo to New York, but when its 30-acre Ohio plant was completed, scheduled for 1984, Fujitec intended to move its global headquarters to Columbus, Ohio.

Establishing an overseas business is like creating a new company. Being "established" at home certainly is no guarantee of success in foreign territory. The companies we have just discussed created a new business strategy because their old one was too unpromising. Interestingly, with their renewed commitment in their new homeland, they have certainly made it.

Being the first one in the market is always important, but being first in Japan is even more so. First, the Japanese tend to view the first in their marketplace as the "original," and this gives the first entrant a status few imitators can match. Second, the peculiar Japanese psychology—a "me-too" mindset—helps assure a huge following if the first-one-in-to-test-the-water catches on. Coca-Cola made a preemptive move to line up distributorship before regulatory restrictions were removed. Its competitors delayed entry by one year until rules regarding foreign investments were changed. That was a quarter of a century ago and no one has caught up with Coca-Cola yet, including the Japanese.

However, the other side of the coin is also true: being first is not necessarily an advantage, since competitors can learn from the pioneer's mistakes. Koji Chiba of Mister Donut recalls his early days of competing against Dunkin' Donuts. While the latter chose its first store in the Ginza, the busiest high-class street in Tokyo, Chiba chose the corner of a supermarket in Mino, a typical suburban town outside of Osaka. His calculation was to make the would-be franchisees even prouder of their location. Looking at Mino, they would say, "I've got better passenger traffic, so I should be able to do better than this location." On the other hand, he thought visitors to Dunkin' Donuts' Ginza shop would say, "Well, this is doing fine. But my location wouldn't compare with this. There's only one Ginza in Japan." So, Chiba kept building model shops in mediocre locations, doing just the opposite of his competitor. His strategy worked.

Joint Venture

Finally, there is a corollary necessity, one which certainly can affect a firm's competitiveness and creative ability to adapt to the idiosyncrasies of the Japanese marketplace. That is the choice of the right partner in a joint venture arrangement. Conflict between partners is one of the biggest reasons behind the withdrawal of foreign firms.

During the 1960s, when most of these joint ventures were consummated, U.S. and European corporations had an absolute technological lead. Their Japanese partners accepted terms and conditions that were not terribly favorable to them in order to get access to advanced technologies and management know-how. However, in the late 1970s two things happened.

One was that most corporations, regardless of origin, suffered serious losses after the energy crisis. Interestingly, most joint venture contracts spelled out how to split the profit, but seldom did they even mention what to do with the losses. So American and European corporations told their Japanese partners that the loss was the result of their management inadequacies, and therefore should be borne entirely by the Japanese. The Japanese partners typically argued that it was, after all, a joint venture, and the loss must be split according to the equity ratio. This kind of discussion had no end and resulted in the partners' serious distrust of each other—only to result in dissolution of the joint venture.

The second trend in the late 1970s was that most Japanese companies, particularly the parent companies, had made remarkable progress in technology and management know-how. By then, it was no longer appropriate to consider the Japanese partner a child and the European or American partner an adult. Most joint venture contracts are written to prohibit international expansion by the Japanese, and their diversification into similar and related fields.

In the meantime, the joint ventures' domestic competitors had emerged as global enterprises with a free hand because they were not bound by the restrictions of a joint venture contract. Komatsu, for example, manufactures con-

struction equipment ranging from power shovels to bulldozers. But Caterpillar–Mitsubishi, a 50–50 joint venture between
Caterpillar Tractor and Mitsubishi Heavy Industries (MHI),
cannot manufacture certain products. For example, hydraulic
excavators are made and distributed by MHI, low-end bulldozers are made by MHI and distributed by the joint venture,
and bulldozers and other earth-moving tractors are made by
the joint venture, and cannot be distributed by MHI! So Komatsu grew from nothing to a $3 billion global giant second
only to Caterpillar, and the Caterpillar–Mitsubishi joint venture's relative position in Japan slipped throughout the past
two decades—from a 1:1 ratio to a 1:3 ratio of sales relative
to Komatsu.

Most American and European corporations in such a situation have not learned how to deal with their partner's growth.
At the same time, the presumed "children" of the relationship
have not learned how to speak up in a truly polished manner.
And so the Japanese develop bad manners to show their frustration. Most joint venture divorces I have seen are the result
of this kind of lack of basic communication. It requires a good
deal of communication to sustain a successful marriage and
even more to keep a corporate marriage—a joint venture—
happy.

On the positive side, the right partnership serves as a
cultural bridge between manufacturer and market. As a case
in point, take General Foods (GF). It tried for more than a
decade to succeed on its own and watched the market share
of its instant coffee (Maxwell) drop from 20 to 14 percent.
Then, in 1975 the firm established a joint venture with Ajinomoto, a food manufacturer, to use the full power of the Japanese partner's product distribution system and personnel and
managerial capabilities. Within two years, Maxwell's share of
the Japanese instant coffee market had recovered. In 1982,
the share was close to 25 percent, a testimony to Ajinomoto's
strong distribution know-how and GF's renewed commitment.

Allstate Life Insurance was able to hurdle the insurance
industry entry restrictions, which stipulate that a new entrant

must provide a new service that will not threaten the viability of any existing industry participant. Allstate's approach was to ally itself with the Seibu Group. Allstate not only acquired a powerful sales channel through this alliance with the retailer, but it also fulfilled the stringent entry requirements by bringing something new to customers—buying insurance over-the-counter.

There are other examples of well-matched ventures: Yokogawa–Hewlett-Packard, a joint venture that is 19 years old; Fuji–Xerox, another 19-year-old liaison; McDonald's, an 11-year-old, 50–50 relationship with Den Fujita; Yamatake–Honeywell, a 45-year-old powerful alliance which has become a true insider in Japan's control components and instrumentation markets. For all of these working alliances, however, there are many that fail. The reasons for dissolution vary from frustration over distribution to changing circumstances.

One should remember that joint ventures should be designed to supplement each partner's shortcoming, and not to exploit each other's strengths and weaknesses. It takes as much effort to make a joint venture a success as to start a grass roots operation and eventually bring it up to a successful level. In both cases, each partner must be fully prepared to dig in and understand customers, competitors, and itself. A joint venture is not a short cut to success. It is a means of resource appropriation and of easing a foreign business's entry to a new terrain. But it should not be viewed as a handy vehicle to reap money without effort, interest, and/or additional resources.

What is the lesson to be learned from the joint venture illustrations? One is that achieving profit potential for Japanese operations may require substantial changes—changes in investment philosophy, changes in organizational alignment, and changes in corporate policies about alliances with outsiders, about decisions to make or to buy components or parts, about autonomy, about unique corporate concepts, and about employee relations.

Many overseas executives feel it is just not worth the effort. "Why should we bother when we are making a satisfactory profit, the way we are now structured?" Another might feel it isn't worth the frustration: "If I'm going to have a nervous breakdown, I'd rather have it at home." On the other hand, many enlightened American executives I know say, "Unless American firms can contain the Japanese by taking a share of their market, we can't expect to beat them at home or anywhere else." And I concur.

The New Wave

By now, the strategic significance of Japan for American and European firms should be fairly obvious. It's the second largest major market for technology-based industries, it's where the competitive threat will come from, it's where much new technology will originate. As competition becomes keener, it's where insurance against neoprotectionism will be needed most.

Some of the more sophisticated U.S. firms in high-technology areas have already moved to Japan to protect their domestic positions. For example, Texas Instruments, which has been producing in Japan since 1968, started production of large-scale integrated circuits in 1980 in Miho, a village north of Tokyo. Motorola has bought out Toko's share of its 50–50 joint venture with Toko and now is the full owner of a plant in Fukushima to produce large-scale integrated circuits, up to 64K RAM. Intel and Analog Devices, Inc. also opened design laboratories and factories in Tsukuba in 1982. GCA, a leading semiconductor equipment maker, revealed joint venture plans with Sumitomo earlier in 1982. IBM, Fairchild, Advanced Micro Devices, and Applied Materials, Inc. have also announced plans to produce very large-scale integrated circuits in Japan.

Tapping Japan's huge market potential and channeling its technological strengths were not the only strategic reasons why many foreign firms moved to Japan. Some entrants admit courting the advantages that can arise from a firm's physical presence on a challenging turf. Xerox is a case in point. When

Japanese entrants in the plain paper copier (PPC) market began shifting from centralized copy centers to lower-speed "convenience" stations, Xerox was able to participate in the rapid development of new technology in low-end PPCs through its joint venture with Fuji. In the face of fierce competition, it stemmed its share erosion and maintained its world leader share in the PPC market.

Thus, becoming a true insider in Japan has the enormous advantage of fending off Japanese competition at home, inside the United States, and in the European Community. The same is true, of course, for the Japanese in the United States and in Europe. And there is no magic to becoming an insider. The success criteria spelled out in the three Cs cannot be overemphasized. And once a firm establishes a true insider position in the Triad, the payoff can be enormous. For an insider, as you have just seen, Japan is not just raw fish and fried vegetables.

PART IV

BECOMING A TRIAD POWER

BY NOW, the strategic significance of Japan, the United States, and Europe should be obvious: This Triad is where the major markets are; it is where the competitive threat comes from; it is where new technologies will originate. As competition becomes keener, it is where preventative action against protectionism will be needed most.

To take advantage of the Triad's markets and forthcoming technologies and to prepare for new competitors, the prime objective of every corporation must be to become a true insider in all three regions.

One caveat must be offered. Lest it be construed that I propose that corporations abandon newly industrialized and developing countries, let me hasten to add that I do not. In truth, the Triad is four-headed (Exhibit IV–1). Each high-technology player participates in the three Triad regions, plus one developing region, to make four: Japan tapping Asia; the Europeans making use of their traditional links in Africa and the Middle East; America selling to her continental neighbors. A solid data base has been assembled to demonstrate the stronger interlinkages of these specific regions. Latin America is the United States' biggest trading partner except for Japan

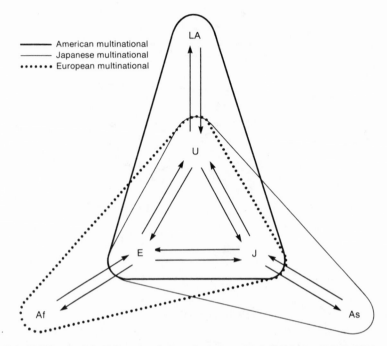

Note: Af, Africa; As, Asia; E, European Community; J, Japan; LA, Latin America; U, United States.

EXHIBIT IV-1   The Triad.

and Europe, and vice versa. Southeast Asia is Japan's biggest trading partner except for the United States and Europe, and vice versa. Africa is the European Community's biggest trading partner except for Japan and the United States, and vice versa.

It should, however, be noted that this "base pattern" may not apply to all industries and to all companies with different historical backgrounds. For many European companies, like Volkswagen and BASF, South America may be more crucial than Africa. For a British company, the ex-members of the Empire, for example, India, Canada, and Australia, may be more important than any other regions. Some American companies depend heavily on the Middle East.

In fact, the Middle East is the common battleground for engineering companies from all three Triad regions for major macroprojects. There, Bechtel, Fluor, and Kellogg (American) might run into competition from Chiyoda, Toyo Engineering Company (TEC), and JGC (Japanese) and Lurgi, Kraftwerk Union (KWU), and Krupp (European).

Each company's activities in the Tetrahedron should be tailored to the company's and its industry's specific priorities and the importance they give to developing in each region. The major point in using this model is to highlight the truly important regions and simplify the corporate view of the world, and avoid having to consider all 150 nations simultaneously, as in the case of the United Nations.

As huge as the market within the Triad base is, and as essential as it might be for high-technology players to succeed in it, the same criteria may not hold true for participants in medium- to low-technology industries. The key factors for success and for failure for Coca-Cola and Pepsi-Cola, for example, are strikingly different from those for IBM or Xerox.

Given that caveat, the importance of being an insider in three Triad markets in order to tap opportunities and counter competition cannot be overstated.

One of the most crucial aspects of the Triad formation is a corporation's ability to get organized to become an insider in each of the critical regions. As we have seen in Chapters 7 and 8, most corporations are organized to serve domestic markets, particularly when the home market is sizable. They are not really placing themselves an equal distance from each of the key markets. I call this the "Anchorage perspective"— symbolically equidistant from Tokyo, New York, and Dusseldorf. Regardless of the corporation's cultural affinity to this Anchorage mentality, it needs to establish a Triad position in order to capitalize on its corporate strengths as well as prepare for an unexpected attack by foreign-affiliated enterprises. Three points should be kept in mind. So in this last part of the book, I will elaborate on the final three points which go into a firm's establishing a true Triad position.

1. The Triad, like it or not, is already forming with such speed, particularly in the high-technology areas, that one cannot stand still and hope that competition on

123

a global scale through syndicated competitors will not hit the particular industry one is in.

2. Developing countries, if organized and approached correctly, can help enormously in strengthening a corporation's global position. But simply treating them as low-wage production centers or as incremental markets will not enhance a corporation's global competitive power.

3. Since many companies cannot actually become a true insider in each of the three Triad regions, alternative solutions, such as consortia and joint ventures, must be sought. However, none of these alternatives will be productive unless the corporation really learns how to communicate institutionally with the very different corporate cultures and languages of other companies. The real challenge, after all, lies in the ability of a corporation to globalize the perspective and language of its headquarters so that it can harmoniously work out both strategic and logistic details in cooperation with yesterday's foes.

9

EMERGENCE OF THE TRIAD

AN EARLY PRESENCE in a new market provides clear advantages. When Tokyo Electric Company first introduced its electronic cash register and began to eat away at National Cash Register's (NCR) market share in Japan, NCR's subsidiary operation in Japan was able to switch from electromechanical to electronic technology to stem the erosion before its domestic position was severely threatened.

As noted earlier, Xerox's preeminence in Japan helped the company anticipate and respond to low-end technology being introduced by Japan. NCR also had "insider" knowledge and experience in Japan, and was thus better able to prepare against the encroachment of Japanese products into its home and world markets than traditional competitors could. Texas Instruments, for example, was able to produce 64K memory chips in Miho (Japan) quickly, while other U.S. companies were fighting off the intrusion of Japanese semiconductor houses into the United States.

In each of these cases, one company was able to adapt quickly because it had an insider position in another strategic part of the Triad.

Now it is wise to remember that new challengers are

less apt to follow established patterns or play the game by traditional rules. In fact, being upstarts or new entrants, they seldom have a vested interest in maintaining the status quo. It will come as no surprise, then, that the vast majority of new patents registered and exchanged among Free World countries are concentrated within five nations: Japan, the United States, West Germany, France, and the United Kingdom. During 1982, these five nations represented 85 percent of the 10,000 patents registered in the world. Furthermore, these countries keep registering their patents in each other's turf to plug their international competitors' unexpected exploitive moves.

However, the pundit who proposed that what the Europeans create, the Americans commercialize and the Japanese copy, is out of date. It is true that Europeans have historically been preeminent in basic research. Without exception laser technology, cryogenics, a majority of inventions underlying the original PPC industry, many technologies in the aerospace industry including fluidics, holography, and more recently X-ray computer tomography (CT) scanners were all originally European efforts. And it is equally true that American entrepreneurship and ability to turn inventive genius into profitable innovation have long been that country's forte. In turn, Japan's application-oriented innovations and its ability to develop products and processes one or two steps further, have enabled it to catch up and, in some instances, take the lead with a sound cost position.

Today, however, innovation and entrepreneurship know no boundaries, and former "also rans" are running neck and neck with yesterday's pacesetters. The scientist who first isolated the interferon gene to help create the science of biotechnology was a Japanese, Dr. Tadatsugu Taniguchi. Masatoshi Shima, then with Busicon and now with Intel, was among the first to put memory and logic chips together in the form known today as the microprocessor. Several U.S. drug firms are following close on the heels of the Swiss and German fermentation-based pharmaceutical leaders, and the Japanese challengers are not too far behind. Europeans, in turn, are making inroads into traditional American strongholds. Siemens and Brown Boveri surprised Westinghouse and General Electric by capturing a significant piece of the U.S. switchgear market. And now, it is Hitachi and Mitsubishi that are surpassing these two European firms in the United States. The French have successfully marketed arms to Latin America and their "Airbus" to Eastern Airlines. The Japanese inroads into specific semiconductor industries has been almost overly documented. Thus, it can be said that in tomorrow's world, the best car possible may very well be of Italian design and it would use German engineering plastics, a Japanese ceramic engine, French steel radial tires, and American microprocessors and power steering, and run on American synthetic fuel.

The relative strengths of these regions also reflect how each spends its R&D money. For example, the United States leads in biotechnology and genetic engineering and specialized semiconductors, Japan in fiber optics, ceramics, and mass produced large-scale integrated circuits, and Europe in chemicals and pharmaceuticals. Japan spends a relatively high portion of its R&D money in such fields as ceramics and steel. The strengths of the German chemical industry are based on where the money is spent.

These expenditures are important in establishing an ongoing process. If a country spends money, and its industry is strong, then it attracts more talented people, which in turn serves its industrial position. This may be too much of a simplification, but doesn't seem to be too far off, given the importance of psychology in attracting people. For example, because of the Ministry of International Trade and Industry's campaign to make Japan "live on silicon," there has been a tremendous shift of the student population to the study of electronics. In 1982, nine of the top ten most popular companies, as ranked by graduating engineering students, were in the electronics industry.

However, only the companies with an insider perspective and knowledge of the three Triad regions can take advantage of the best and the strongest industries in each area.

New Approaches

The lesson taught by new contenders has been well internalized by today's alert corporations. Many American and not a few European corporations are now moving in a variety of ways to challenge Japan on its own turf and vice versa. The approaches range from grass roots operations to a loose consortium of "distant" competitors. This very activity is, in itself, a force of change.

International cooperation is not new, but the pattern of intricate liaisons now taking shape is unprecedented. This pattern is altering the structure of traditional and new industries. Let us take a look at the importance of these liaisons in the Triad in several key industries in more detail.

Collaboration in the Auto Industry

Collaboration is most prevalent in small car production. None of the Detroit's Big Three (Chrysler, Ford, and General Motors), is purely an American corporation. General Motors recently boosted its equity in Isuzu—ranked sixth among Japan's 11 automakers—to 34 percent. Cars manufactured in Japan under the GM label will be distributed by Isuzu through its dealerships. In a joint venture between the two firms, GM will take over the distribution of Isuzu-built subcompacts and trucks in the United Kingdom, Western Europe, and Africa. General Motors dealers will continue to handle distribution in the United States and Canada. General Motors also has a 5 percent share in Suzuki Motors, from which it is gleaning minicar technology and for which it serves as a marketing arm in the States. This gives GM an indirect link to Volvo, which also owns a piece of Suzuki, and a relationship—twice removed—with Renault, which has 10 percent equity in Volvo.

Additionally, GM has seven other affiliate companies in Europe as well as a piece of Australia's major car distributor, known as GM–Holden. But that's not all. General Motors is working with Hitachi to develop a microcomputer-based electronic system for a new line of fuel-efficient GM cars, and it is involved with a joint venture in state-of-the art robotics with Fujitsu–Fanuc.

Perhaps the most significant tie-up is the one that GM has worked out with Toyota. It wants to lure the Japanese car maker into its idle California plants to make 200,000 small passenger cars a year. Since GM already has a tie-up with two smaller Japanese automakers, why Toyota? Probably because the sales of its 1,800-cc J car—introduced in 1981 to compete in the small car war—have made slow headway.

Some skeptics view the GM–Toyota alliance as more Machiavellian than strategic. They contend that Toyota deliberately chose GM as its partner in the hope that the U.S. Justice Department's Antitrust Division would challenge the arrangement. (The two companies' combined share of the world market was over 20 percent in 1983; together they produced more than 8.0 million cars.) Meanwhile, so this line of speculation runs, Toyota has chalked up some easy goodwill mileage in the trade battle.

This rationale ignores the fact that Ford, not GM, was Toyota's first choice. It also does not reflect insight into Toyota's timidness in going overseas on its own, as discussed in Chapter 7.

In any event, now that the tie-up with Toyota is approved, GM would have a range of small cars to offer. Toyota, on the other hand, would be gaining a strong production foothold in the United States. Whether or not it could transfer its culturally bound *kanban* production and just-in-time sourcing systems to the States is an entirely open question. Traditionally, the Mikawa-based Japanese automobile giant has concentrated its production facilities and vendors in a 20-kilometer radius of Toyota City, in Aichi Prefecture. Its centralized production system has made Toyota one of the most efficient producers of cars.

But it is also true that its approach is an Achilles heel when it comes to production abroad. Toyota has never produced a car in Tokyo or in Kyushu. Unlike Nissan's decentralized approach of having plants all over the country, Toyota has been very reluctant to produce its cars away from the province of Mikawa. Its monotonous and cautious approach has made it an excellent company in terms of stability but its domestic orientation and lack of cosmopolitan management will continue to haunt the company as it attempts to shift the upstream (engineering and production) portion of the business system abroad, particularly to the United States and Europe.

One has to remember that at Toyota the English-speaking staff has been traditionally treated as lightweight specialists, and the smell of soy sauce reigned over that of butter. The reason why it was so successful in exporting its high-quality cars was simply because the soy sauce culture of the manufacturer, Toyota Motor Company (TMC), was shunned by the sister company Toyota Motor Sales (TMS), which handled all the marketing and exports until the two companies merged in 1982.

The new company is therefore the mixture of two different cultures. If the TMC culture dominates over TMS, then it will be a long while before Toyota has a successful full business system in Europe and the United States. In my personal opinion, the joint venture with GM in the United States was therefore as much to meet Toyota's needs as those of GM. The biggest remaining question is how the two giant—and excellent—companies, with completely different cultures, can develop a common language of communication.

The outcome of the joint venture will not be known until the end of this decade, but it will certainly provide one of the best experiments on how different "corporate blood types" can accomplish a successful transfusion.

In any event, whatever the arrangement between Toyota and GM, it is likely to trigger still further liaisons among other challengers in the industry. Right now, for example, Ford Motor Company owns 24.4 percent of Japan's number three car maker, Toyo Kogyo (Mazda). Out of this tie-up has emerged a Japanese-made minicar which is basically Toyo Kogyo's "Familia" model with a facelift. Ford dealers will push this car in Australia and Latin America. Meanwhile, some 20 Japanese companies have recently established a corporation, called Autorama, to market the small car and other Ford brands domestically in Japan. Toyo Kogyo also supplies Ford with engines.

But Ford has not limited its Japanese involvement to Toyo Kogyo. It has designated six Japanese manufacturers as prequalified suppliers to its stateside plants. These suppliers of transmission cases, oil seals, and other components include two Toshiba plants, Nippon Electric Company (NEC), and three lesser-known Japanese firms. Ford's European operations include assembly plants in England and West Germany (Fordwerke), Belgium, and Spain.

As for Chrysler Corporation, it owns 15 percent of Mitsubishi Motors, Japan's fourth-place runner-up. Chrysler is seeking a production partnership in which the Tokyo-based firm will produce cars in Japan to be sold in the States, under such brand names as Colt, Sapporo, and Challenger. The Chrysler–Mitsubishi liaison, which goes back to the 1960s, is an example of an old relationship entering a new phase. Originally, Chrysler helped redesign Mitsubishi's Gallant, which it then distributed in the United States as the Dodge Colt. Today, Chrysler proposes to send design and production teams to Mitsubishi's plants to learn modern processes and quality control techniques.

Chrysler is linked to Europe through France's Peugeot (Chrysler owns 15 percent of Peugeot's stock) and West Germany's Volkswagen, which supplies engines to Chrysler.

American Motor Company's (AMC's) foreign relationship is more direct. American Motor Company sold 49.9 percent of its equity to France's Renault for some $400 million. The child of the three-year affair between AMC and Renault is a French-designed and engineered subcompact named—appropriately—the Alliance. Although the car is being manufactured by AMC's Wisconsin plant, half the components are French-made. American Motor Company's French alliance, however, does not affect its agreement with Mitsubishi Motors. The latter is producing the CD-3 jeep in Japan.

131

A more concrete picture of the automobile industry's intricate network of international relationships is shown in Exhibit 9–1. What is the significance of this enormously complex Triad development? Are these the signs of weakness? The answer is clearly no. These are the realities of the contemporary world. These are not bad signs. This behavior on the part of Detroit's Big Three reflects very logical and sound business judgment. What is odd is the perception this behavior gives to the American people in general, which is that Detroit is fighting against Japan, Inc. Actually, there has been no other time in the history of the two nations when a relationship at the private-company level has been as close and interdependent as today. Therefore, we simply have to develop our ears and eyes despite the media-created picture of "trade friction" between the two nations.

Computer Microchip Crossovers

Collaboration and direct participation are equally as apparent in the new generation of key industries. Consider the computer industry and its basic subcomponent, the microchip, the manufacture of which is an integral part of the business of many leading computer producers. International Business Machines (IBM), Control Data Corporation (CDC), Hewlett-Packard (HP), Burroughs Corporation, Data General Corporation (DGC), and Digital Equipment Corporation (DEC) in the United States all have captive microchip facilities, as do all of Japan's mainframe producers. A graphic illustration of the shifting of this industry toward Triad consortia is shown in Exhibit 9–2. The interlinkage is so complex that I had to pull out the consortia based on "technical tie-ups" separately in Exhibit 9–3. There are dozens of negotiations currently underway, so I am pretty sure these charts will become outdated in a few years.

When Amdahl Corporation took on IBM in the mainframe market in 1975, it was backed by Fujitsu. In exchange for its 30 percent stake, the Japanese firm got technical exposure.

Today Fujitsu is a formidable competitor. In addition to supplying Amdahl's central processing units and sharing semiconductor technology with the California-based firm, Fujitsu has design centers in California. It also took a 51 percent share with TRW, in TFC, Inc. which handles the marketing of various Fujitsu systems in the United States through a direct sales force, but the venture ended in 1983. In Europe, Fujitsu has a contract to furnish technology to Britain's ICL and an original equipment manufacturing arrangement with Siemens AG in Germany. This alliance is natural, because Fujitsu is an offspring of Fuji Electric, which was founded in 1926 as a 50–50 joint venture between Baron Furukawa and Baron Siemens. Siemens, in turn, has purchased several U.S. firms, mostly in the semiconductor area, to establish a beachhead in the United States.

In three other computer consortia, American and Japanese firms have interests in each other's strategic spheres of influence in Europe.

Control Data Corporation has joint ventures with Britain's ICL and West Germany's Nixdorf and equity in Belgium's nationalized computer company. In Japan, CDC has (in addition to its own sales subsidiary) a tie-up with Takeda Riken, which supplies its logic and memory testers as well as a cross-licensing agreement with Hitachi.

Hitachi, in turn, has a "technical cooperation" agreement to loan Hewlett-Packard its 64K RAM technology, and it supplies IBM-compatible large-scale computers to National Advanced System Corporation (NASCO), a subsidiary of National Semiconductor Corporation which, in turn, markets them in the United States. Hitachi also has a semiconductor plant in West Germany, a technological tie-up with ICL, and a California-based semiconductor design center.

The second major consortium includes the non-IBM-compatible group of companies, centered around Honeywell Information Systems (HIS) which exchanges technology and has a joint venture arrangement with NEC, Japan's number one semiconductor and computer maker. Honeywell Information Systems also had a 47 percent stake in Bull, France's national-

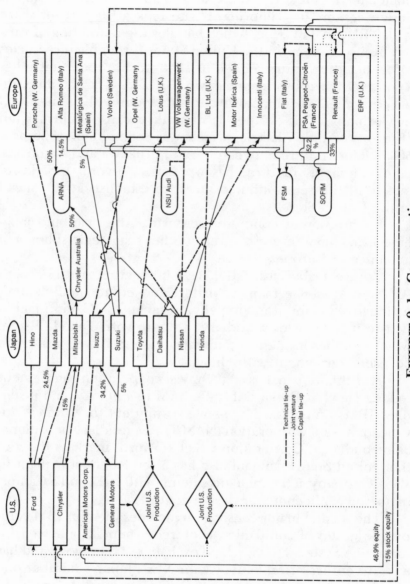

EXHIBIT 9-1 Car consortia.

134

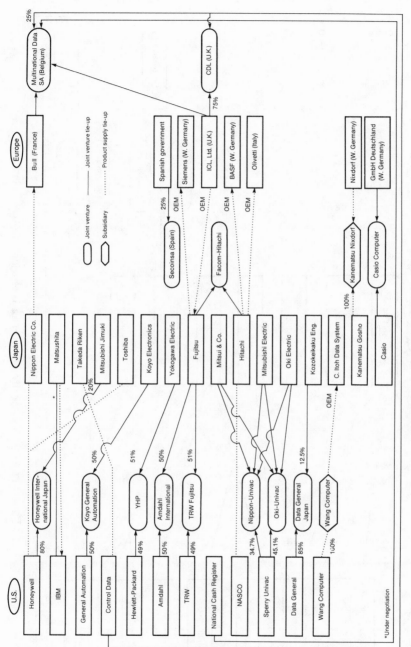

EXHIBIT 9-2 Computer consortia.

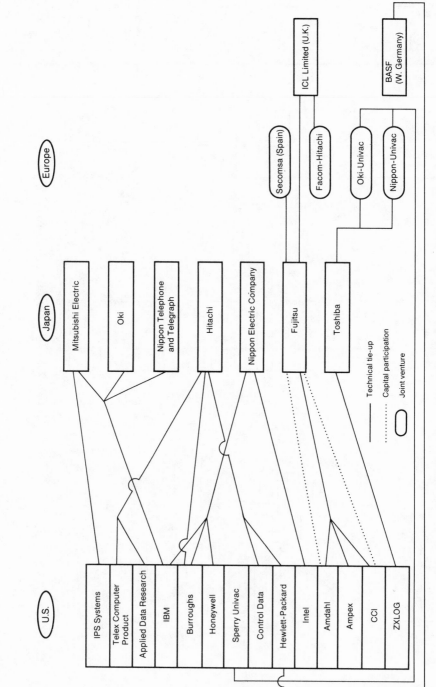

EXHIBIT 9-3 Computer consortia technical tie-ups.

136

ized computer company (but this share is now about 9 percent), and a joint venture tie-up with CDC to manufacture magnetic peripherals. The Japanese member of this consortium, NEC, also has a technical tie-up with Bull, a semiconductor plant in the United Kingdom, and is currently planning to establish an integrated circuit design center in Sunnyvale, California.

The third computer group includes Sperry Rand's UNIVAC, which has been indirectly linked to Japan for over a decade through a joint venture in which UNIVAC has a 45 percent share, Oki Electric the lion's share of 46.92 percent, and Mitsubishi Electric an 8 percent share. In June 1983, however, Sperry and Mitsubishi announced a five-year collaborative agreement in which the two firms would swap computer technology—Sperry tapping into Mitsubishi's small and medium-sized know-how and Mitsubishi gaining Sperry's large-scale experience. The collaboration agreement covers development, production, and marketing.

And what of IBM? This former loner is now exchanging computer patents with NTT in exchange for semiconductor and electronic-telephone switching patents. In 1982, IBM's Japanese subsidiary contracted with Oki to produce *kanji* printers. Though IBM has previously ordered Japanese components, this was the first time IBM purchased a finished product from a Japanese manufacturer. Furthermore, in June of 1982, unconfirmed word leaked out to the press that IBM was entering into a joint venture agreement with Matsushita to develop and market a personal computer, marketed in Japan as the 5550 Multistation—a personal computer (PC), terminal, and word processor in one.

IBM also went into a series of joint ventures in Japan. It formed a three-way venture with Mitsubishi Corporation and Cosmo-80 to enter into the value-added network business. It also acquired one third of the equity of Japan Business Computer to jointly develop products as well as to distribute low-end computers. These dynamic moves signify IBM's commitment to become a true insider in Japan.

IBM's phenomenal success with its PC in the United States

could not have come without its in-depth understanding of the many high-quality vendors of electronics devices in the Japanese computer industry. As is well known, IBM's PC strategy is based on the concept of "orchestrating the entire business system," but not producing everything for the system on its own, as had been the case with Big Blue up to that point.

In other words, IBM's PC is made of the best of all worlds: Intel processors which originate from Hitachi, an Epson printer, and a TDK power supply—all from Japan; Tanden and Shugart disk drives, Keytronics and AMP for IBM-designed keyboards, and SCI Systems motherboard—from the United States; and an Atlas monitor from Hong Kong. IBM's PC is also sold by a group of third party companies, such as the consumer-retail experts of Sears Roebuck and Computer Land. Its Japanese twin, IBM Multistation, uses an Oki printer, an Alps keyboard, and a Matsushita monitor. IBM's flexible policy regarding the sources of its components and its willingness to both make and buy components put the traditional Japanese electronics houses to shame. To put a final touch to these aggressive moves in Japan, IBM announced in July 1984 the formation of the Asia Pacific Group. The APG is a leg of the Triad which accommodates over 150 corporate staff in Tokyo from the worldwide IBM organization. In short, it is the headquarters responsible for Japan and the rest of Asia and Oceania.[1]

In the more specialized field of semiconductors, there is a new Triad consortia in silicon wafers consisting of Japan's Shinetsu, America's Monsanto and Dow Corning, and West Germany's Wacker Chemie.[2] Although not finalized, the proposed consortia virtually includes all of the old business foes of the silicon single-crystal industry in a joint participation in Wacker Chemie's Oregon plant. Wacker, of course, is a member of West Germany's mighty Hoechst group; it produces 2,000 tons of polycrystal silicon a year in its Burghausen plant, and converts it to single-crystal wafers. The formation of this consortia (Exhibit 9–4) means that the three traditional competitors from all corners of the Triad (Shinetsu, Monsanto,

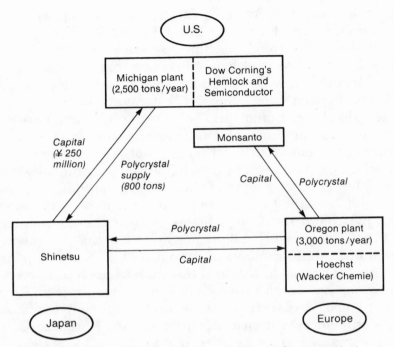

EXHIBIT 9–4 Silicon wafer consortia under negotiation.

Source: Data from *Japan Economic Journal*, February 19, 1984.

and Wacker) are now joining hands to operate the raw materials plant in Oregon.

This sampling of technology, production, and distribution exchanges ought to puncture the traditional perceptions of competitive behavior. There are even more Triad-shaped agreements between partners in Japan, the United States, and Europe in the fields of robotics, aerospace, biotechnology, and carbon fibers (Exhibits 9–5 through 9–8). Similar consortia are emerging in computer-aided design/computer-aided manufacturing with GE–Hitachi and Aida–Estel, and in ethical drugs with Smith, Kline, and French–Fujisawa–Ciba–Geigy, and Bayer–Takeda–Abbott. In the communications industry, American Telephone and Telegraph is now moving into Europe by joining hands with Olivetti and Philips. Plessey, the

British equivalent of Western Electric, has tied up with Nitsuko in Japan and Burroughs in the United States.

It should be noted that there are relatively few United States–Europe tie-ups. I have to confess that this impression might be due to my lack of understanding of the negotiations going on between the European Community and the United States. However, it might also be that American and Japanese companies are finding each other more valuable in these high-technology areas, and that they are not really studying the European possibilities. Conversely, European companies may feel defensive about some of their traditional industries and are a bit hesitant to reach out and form new syndications with Japan and the United States. A recent announcement of AT&T's tie-up with Philips and Olivetti might spur another round of fresh assessments of Euro-American ventures.

Another possible reason is that most blue chip American companies have their own subsidiaries in the European Community, and vice versa. Looking at the cumulative amount of investment by American companies in the European Community and by European companies in the United States (Exhibit 9–9), this hypothesis is probably true, at least for the traditional industries. And it should also be noted from this analysis that Japan has been somewhat of a blind spot for American and European companies. While money is not everything, these cumulative investments eloquently demonstrate many corporations' inability to view all three regions as parts of an equally weighted Triad.

My point here in mentioning the lack of United States–European Community consortia relationships, however, is still valid. I would like to see more fresh, unencumbered appraisals of American opportunities in Europe and of Europeans' opportunities in the United States in high-technology areas. Companies that depend on their own foreign subsidiaries are not accustomed to looking at the newer possibilities of forming a consortium with yesteryear's foes, or with a total stranger. Psychologically they may be used to viewing each other from the viewpoints of their own subsidiaries. In any event, I would assert that a fresh look at all possible relationships across all

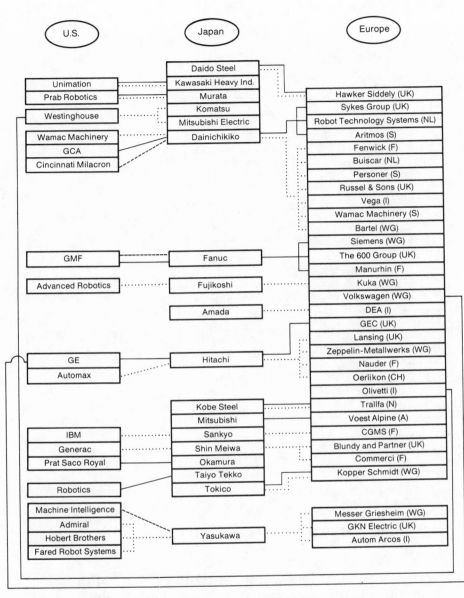

U.S.   Japan   Europe

U.S.	Japan	Europe
	Daido Steel	
Unimation	Kawasaki Heavy Ind.	
Prab Robotics	Murata	Hawker Siddely (UK)
Westinghouse	Komatsu	Sykes Group (UK)
	Mitsubishi Electric	Robot Technology Systems (NL)
Wamac Machinery	Dainichikiko	Aritmos (S)
GCA		Fenwick (F)
Cincinnati Milacron		Buiscar (NL)
		Personer (S)
		Russel & Sons (UK)
		Vega (I)
		Wamac Machinery (S)
		Bartel (WG)
		Siemens (WG)
GMF	Fanuc	The 600 Group (UK)
		Manurhin (F)
Advanced Robotics	Fujikoshi	Kuka (WG)
		Volkswagen (WG)
	Amada	DEA (I)
		GEC (UK)
		Lansing (UK)
		Zeppelin-Metallwerks (WG)
GE	Hitachi	Nauder (F)
Automax		Oerlikon (CH)
		Olivetti (I)
	Kobe Steel	Trallfa (N)
	Mitsubishi	Voest Alpine (A)
IBM	Sankyo	CGMS (F)
Generac	Shin Meiwa	Blundy and Partner (UK)
Prat Saco Royal	Okamura	Commerci (F)
	Taiyo Tekko	Kopper Schmidt (WG)
Robotics	Tokico	
Machine Intelligence		Messer Griesheim (WG)
Admiral		GKN Electric (UK)
Hobert Brothers	Yasukawa	Autom Arcos (I)
Fared Robot Systems		

———— Technical links ············ Sales links ---------- Joint venture

Abbreviations: A, Austria; Ch, Switzerland; F, France; I, Italy; N, Norway; NL, Netherlands; S, Sweden; U.K., United Kingdom; W.G., West Germany)

EXHIBIT 9–5   Robotics consortia.

141

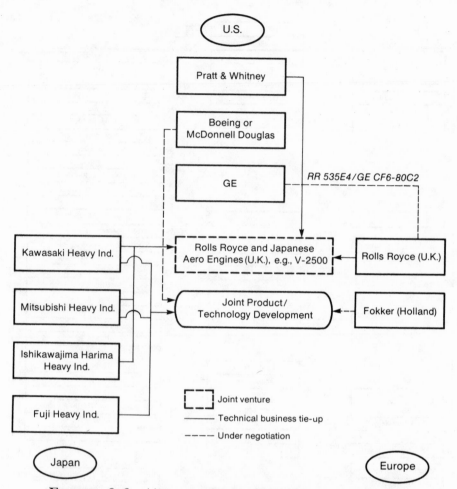

EXHIBIT 9–6   Air transport consortia (XJB and YXX plan).

three Triad regions would be an eye-opening experience. I personally think it is a shame that United States–European Community consortium formation, particularly in the new industrial areas, is not taking on a more dynamic character.

A 1982 study by The Conference Board[3] called the Triad phenomenon "intriguing": Of the top 50 firms in the United States that derived 50 percent or more of their total revenues from foreign activities, the study said, 40 percent had equal or minority partnerships with foreign affiliates. These partner-

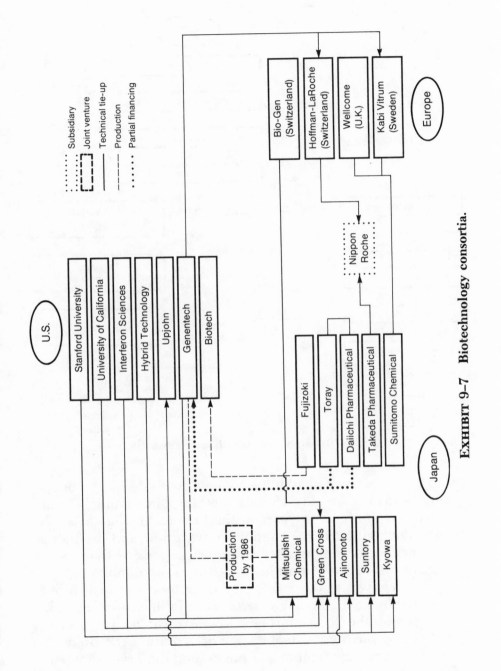

EXHIBIT 9-7 Biotechnology consortia.

143

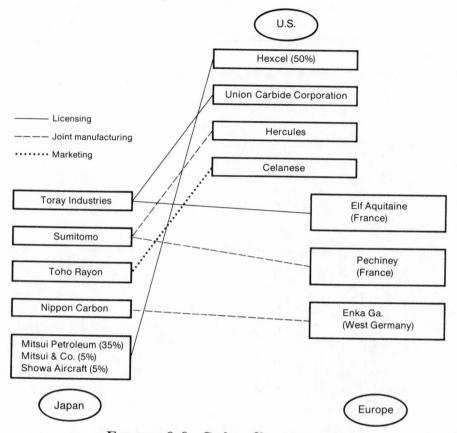

EXHIBIT 9–8 Carbon fibers consortia.

ship ventures were in addition to their own subsidiaries operating abroad. In reality there is nothing "intriguing" about it. Rather, the basis is clear. In the high-technology area, in particular, the R&D for coming up with new and profitable products has become riskier and more expensive than ever. Once developed, one must leverage the new technology more than ever, even at the risk of reducing its theoretical profit potential by giving up a few parts of the business system and/ or regions. If the R&D effort fails, a company must still survive, perhaps by buying the technology or acquiring the product. These are the fundamental reasons behind the Triad consortia formation.

Cumulative total at the end of fiscal 1982
Unit: $1 million

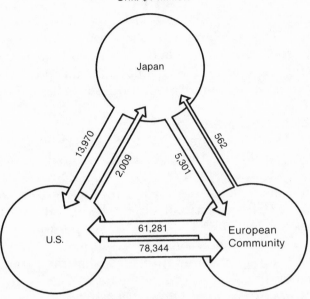

Remarks: 1. Japan-United States and Japan-European Community figures represent cumulative totals as of end of fiscal 1982 on authorization and registration bases.
2. European Community figures represent total for ten nations. However, in the case of European direct investment in Japan, figure represents total for six countries (West Germany, Britain, France, the Netherlands, Belgium, and Denmark).

EXHIBIT 9–9 Investment interchange among Japan, the United States, and the European Community. (Cumulative total at the end of fiscal 1982; unit: $1 million)

Source: Data from Bank of Japan, Survey of Current Business, as quoted by Masuo Shibata, "Looking Together for Tomorrow's World," *Journal of Japanese Trade and Industry*, No. 11984, pp. 19–24.

Thus, my purpose in sharing the catalogue of consortia, as I have done in this chapter, is twofold. First, I want to highlight the high degree of collaboration now taking place. Second, I would like to illustrate the strategic response of medium- and high-technology firms in coping with the new currents of change which I elaborated in Part I of this book.

These activities differ from the merger mania of the 1960s and early 1970s in three very important ways. First, consider the form of the current phenomenon. For the most part, this involves a loose alliance of distant competitors; mergers reflected a consolidation of close competitors. Second, the thrust is different. The current activity is more international in spirit and scope. Former mergers, although transnational—especially within the European Community—were often unfriendly and sometimes incompatible. Finally, the consequences are different. The current consortia and starting activities encourage dynamic competition; mergers tended to choke it.

Consider the unsuccessful transnational mergers—Estel (Hoesch Hoogovens), Fokker–VFW, and Dunlop–Pirelli. On the other hand, the Airbus consortium—British Aerospace, French Aerospatiale, Deutsche Airbus, and Spanish Construcciones Aeronauticas—has shown some evidence of success: a competitive aircraft was built, although at great cost. Similarly, the Agfa–Gevaert merger seems to be operating effectively.

In contrast, recent consortia are moving away from the mode of traditional competitors by sharing resources and swapping products to avert development risks. *Instead of geographically close competitors joining forces, the current trend is for distant competitors to merge and share functions such as R&D and production.* British Leyland produces a medium-sized Honda in the United Kingdom, and Nissan produces certain Volkswagen models in Japan, and vice versa.

Even in the case of direct operation, emphasis has shifted from developing countries to the Triad regions. Locating a major plant, and thereby establishing an insider presence, has become a must in order for a company to survive in the fiercely competitive medium- to high-technology industries.

Compare the following cases with generally accepted competitive behavior. American manufacturers are invading Japan's semiconductor domain to better arm themselves for the fierce rivalry ahead. Intel and Analog Devices, Inc, opened laboratories near Tokyo in 1983. GCA, one of the world's largest semiconductor equipment makers, revealed joint venture plans with Sumitomo earlier in 1984. Fairchild, Advanced Micro Devices, and Applied Materials, Inc., have also announced to manufacture very large integrated circuits (VLSIs) in Japan. Even IBM has joined the fray and plans to make VLSIs in Yasu, Japan.

This movement into a competitor's home turf is not limited to specialized semiconductor makers. It includes the "Pentagon family" of firms, which produce high-performance integrated circuits. Hughes Aircraft, Rockwell International, and TRW, Inc. want to capitalize on Japanese production strengths and market their high-quality large-scale integrated circuits to the Japanese market. These moves, of course, make arguments against Japanese VLSIs, based on U.S. national security interests, somewhat unreasonable.

Corning Glass in the spring of 1982 announced its purchase of RCA Research Laboratories, a subsidiary of RCA Corporation in Japan, where it plans to establish a new optical fiber R&D facility. Meanwhile, Furukawa Electric Company has obtained working rights to Corning's patent and has given Sumitomo Electric Industries, Ltd. sublicensing rights. Some industry-watchers speculate that these moves are a prelude to a more intimate relationship.

To tap America's strength in cable television technology, Sony America is conducting R&D on new-type cable televisions in the United States. In fact, there is no corresponding division in Sony's headquarters in Japan. Matsushita is strengthening R&D coordination between its U.S. subsidiaries and Japan. Likewise, IBM is designing and producing products exclusively for the Japanese market in Japan.

More publicized moves include Honda Motor Company's new automobile assembly plant in Ohio as well as its successful cooperation with British Leyland; Fujitec Company's new headquarters in New York and sparkling new elevator and escalator plant in Ohio; Nissan's greenfield plant near Memphis; and Hitachi's second color television plant in California.

In Europe, NEC has announced it will produce microchips in Scotland. Fujitsu Fanuc Ltd. has a facility under construction in Luxemburg which will make complex production control systems. These companies are experiencing the same competitive pressures that led forerunners like Sony, Matsushita, Yoshida Kogyo Kabushiki Kaisha (zippers), Toshiba, Nihon Seiko Kabushiki Kaisha (NSK) (bearings), Honda, and others to become insiders in the difficult markets of the European Community.

These are all moves reflecting leading-edge companies' realization that they have to become fully familiar with each of the Triad regions. Whether or not a corporation can achieve this direct (or, through partnership, effective indirect) presence is a matter of vital importance. No matter how difficult or unpleasant the task may be, one has to establish an effective insider position if one is to be successful in Triad markets consisting of 600 million people.

10

THE ROLE OF THE
DEVELOPING REGIONS

SEVERAL FRIENDS OF MINE, who had gone over the synopis of this book, told me I could be interpreted as being a neocolonialistic capitalist by my stressing the importance of the Triad regions. I am fully aware of the danger of being labeled as such. Nonetheless, as a consultant who gives advice to major world corporations, I cannot divert their attention away from the critical need to face the realities of the contemporary world.

One of the reasons many large West German companies are faced with the rapid decay of their global competitiveness is that they went into the lucrative developing regions in Latin America, the Middle East, and Africa where the competition was weak and the local government hospitable. During the 1970s, when these companies had a lot of money to invest, they built gigantic plants in the jungles and bought unrelated and/or culturally dissimilar companies in the United States and Europe. They should have been investing in advancing their mainstream technology and becoming true insiders in Japan and the United States.

The penalties they are paying now are enormous. The catch-up costs in outfitting these plants with automation, electronics, robotics, and computers are astronomical and may never be recovered. Furthermore, many of the precious operations they successfully built up in the developing regions have become unprofitable, either because of the incursions by competitive Japanese and American firms, or because of economic discontinuities due to the unexpected changes in government. Fixing these problems, no matter how small the country's market potential may be, gives the headquarters' management about the same degree of headache, in terms of political and social sensitivities, as having to send in the top-level corporate troubleshooters or "fire fighters," as I have termed them.

I cannot, therefore, recommend that major corporations try to escape from facing the realities of the business world. If a company has a strong and cozy position in any developing region, fine. Keep it. But such a company should not expect its subsidiaries to substantially contribute to the enhancement of its global competitive position, unless the company has initiated a series of actions directed at its becoming a true Triad power.

Now, this brings us back to the original question of what to do in (and with) the developing regions. Some scholars (and even my colleagues) argue that developing countries are where the future is. That's where the major population growth is. Right. But if one goes a step further in that direction, the argument rapidly becomes shaky. For example, the GNP represented by the three Triad regions in 1960 was 75 percent of the Free World economy, in 1970 it was 73 percent, and today is 72 percent. That's a very small diminution over 20 years.

You couldn't profitably reflect such slow structural changes in developing a corporate strategy. Furthermore, the slippage of the two percentage points in the 1960s is entirely due to Europe. On aggregate, both Japan and the United States have grown faster than the developing and less-developed regions. Despite the slippage, Europe still represents 25 percent of the global GNP, and is one of the world's three most critical and sophisticated markets.

Furthermore, these macroeconomic data are often mis-leading in formulating a corporation's global strategies. As is well known, the European Community's slow growth was be-cause of the United Kingdom in the 1960s and more recently because of France. The United States' slow growth is a net result of the declining Midwest and East and the rapidly grow-ing West and Sunbelt. Of the rapidly growing states, California alone is bigger than Brazil, and Texas's "gross state product" is bigger than the combined GNP of the Association of South-east Asian Nations (ASEAN) countries. IBM, as a corporation, has sales of $40 billion, and net value-added sales of $25 billion. And that is half the size of the net value-added, or gross domes-tic product, of the Republic of China. And these regions and companies in the Triad are growing much more rapidly than the so-called developing regions.

To reiterate, Japan is a combination of growth industries and decaying ones. Simply because its GNP growth has come down to a 4 percent level from the traditional 10 to 20 percent level doesn't mean the growth opportunities in Japan have ended. It has dozens of large and dynamic industries that are doubling their size year in, year out. These are the indus-tries with high value-added increments and high potential payout. If one classifies an industry by value added, one can conclude that, while low value-added products are shifting their production base to less-developed countries (LDCs), the high value-added products are still produced and consumed in the Triad (Exhibit 10–1). Naturally, these high value-added product lines represent better profit-making potential than medium to low value-added old-line products.

The profit potential would be less if Triad countries, with their higher wage rate, tried to stay in undifferentiated, low value-added industries. Metal bending and forging businesses, in general, have become unattractive in the Triad. Even diesel engines and color televisions have become unprofitable. They have become what my Cleveland colleague, Elliot Ross, called "engineered commodities" in his McKinsey staff paper, "Mak-ing Money with Proactive Pricing," August 1983. These are the quasi-technology-based industries which, indeed, do re-

151

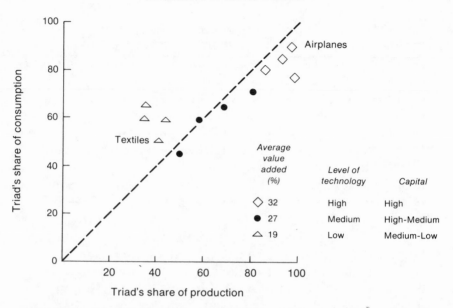

EXHIBIT 10–1   The Triad's share of production and consumption (percent). Most high-technology products are still produced and consumed in the Triad.

quire a high degree of engineering sophistication in design and production. However, they are not difficult and sophisticated enough to stay beyond the reach of new producers. In fact, newly industrialized countries (NICs), such as Korea, Taiwan, Mexico, Hong Kong, and Singapore, can produce these products. So if a producer of these goods is located in one of the high-wage Triad countries and cannot advance the art of design and/or production by a quantum leap, then there is no profit potential. These industries are "structurally troubled," because the price level of the industry will be dictated by the low cost producers in NICs. If one tries to raise the price artificially, it can also invite domestic "me too" competitors, because everyone in depressed industries is looking for easy and profit-making diversification opportunities.

The golden combination in these "engineered commodity" businesses is to produce in low-wage countries on a large scale with state-of-the-art production technologies. Often,

Triad corporations enter low-wage countries with a large variable-cost structure, primarily in search of low-cost labor. The American textile industry has a history of migrating in search of a low-wage labor force without really changing the modus operandi of the industry itself. Over the past century, it moved from New England to the Appalachian Mountains, and then to Japan, Korea, and Taiwan in the 1960s. During the 1970s, it migrated farther south to Indonesia, the Philippines, India, and Sri Lanka. In each place, it created hope during the first five years and problems during the second five years, only to continue to look for a solution to its problems by moving to a site farther south. Maybe, in the 1990s, the textile industry will end up in the People's Republic of China, and the one billion people there will help it find its eternal home.

A company that migrates in search of low-cost labor typically has a competitive half-life of only five years, no matter how hard it looks for a stable haven. Unskilled labor forces available for low prices in the developing countries are by definition "general purpose." If Singapore is rumored to be the best place to assemble consumer electronics, everyone moves in. This was the case in the early 1970s. But a company can only recruit able management talent by means of money, thus raising white-collar salaries rapidly.

Singapore's national sport is "job hopping." You might think this is inevitable since 70 percent of Singapore population consists of Overseas Chinese. It is their nature to constantly look for a better job, and ultimately work for their family business. Nonetheless, the degree to which job hopping is a problem there far exceeds such Confucian and Chinese-based economies as Hong Kong and Taiwan. The problem can only be attributable to the rapid expansion of the economy—far beyond its ability to create a commensurate number of qualified managers. Viewed from the perspective of a country like Japan, where managers seldom move, a long-term investment in people and facilities of major magnitude in Singapore is out of the question, unless this particular problem is curbed.

In a situation like this, blue-collar workers also rapidly

153

are at a premium, and their wages start rising to reflect the rising standard of living and competitive job markets, as briefly discussed in Chapter 1 (see discussion on the expense of cheap labor). Singapore's response to this was to import low-cost labor from Malaysia, India, and Sri Lanka as seen in their numerous shipyards in Jurong.

Despite these efforts, multinational "migrating birds" will recognize the difficulties, and casually transfer their plants to Johor (across the channel from Singapore) or to Colombo. In other words, they move into labor-exporting countries to take advantage of the "no airfare" and "no fringes" policies for indigenous workers.

Matsushita has done something completely contrary to what is dictated by this conventional wisdom. The company built an advanced world-class compressor plant in Singapore comparable to their Japanese facility, with an annual through-put capacity of 3,000,000 units. This plant is aimed at not only the ASEAN, but also the Middle East, Europe, and the United States. Since it has the low-labor-cost advantage of Singapore compared with the Triad, and of the economies of scale in addition to the state-of-the-art production facility, it was an easy victory for Matsushita to use this plant to penetrate the traditionally very difficult U.S. market. Today, Matsushita sells over 30 percent of low-end compressors consumed in the United States for refrigerators.

Matsushita has another success story based on a similar strategy for its air conditioner plant in the Selangor District of Malaysia. Here, again, the company built a state-of-the-art production plant comparable to its main factory in Japan. With access to the labor at one tenth the Japanese rate—despite Malaysia's productivity rate of one half that of Japan—the company was able to produce air conditioners at the lowest cost in this geographical region.

This kind of serious commitment to developing nations gives the Asian region some hope. I have been personally involved in a number of industrial policy-making councils in Asia. One of the agonies I went through was the lack of effective solutions to the widening disparity in income between

the northern and southern countries—the so called "North–
South problem." The per capita income difference, with in-
comes in the northern countries being five to ten times greater
than those in the southern countries, has not changed over
the past decade.

In fact, resource-based countries like the members of the
Organization of Petroleum Exporting Countries, Malaysia, and
Indonesia are heavily influenced by the cyclical nature of commodity prices. These countries have difficulty training enough
qualified people to convert their entire economies so they
will be more like those of value-added, industrial nations.
Countries like Thailand and the Philippines, with few natural
resources, are still heavily dependent on primary industry exports, such as rubber, sugar, and palm oil, which suffer from
the price volatility problem because they are natural
resources. Thus, these countries serve as the providers of
raw materials for the Triad nations' industrial might. In this
context, Australia and New Zealand are not very different
from these developing countries because they are also heavily dependent on natural resources exports to the Triad.
"If Japan sneezes, ASEAN catches pneumonia" is not an exag-
geration.

Likewise the NICs face their own problems. They have
grown by taking the labor-rich portion of the secondary industries away from the Triad. They used to import key components from the Triad, add labor, and then export the final
assembly back to the Triad nations. For example, in the semiconductor industry, these countries do not have the capital-
intensive upstream process which is known as "clean room"
operations. After ions are implanted and diffused on silicon
wafers in the clean room, the semiconductor microchips are
flown to the Philippines and Malaysia where they go through
the labor-intensive operations of bonding, assembling, and
packaging. Newly industrialized countries like Taiwan, Korea,
Hong Kong, and Singapore then buy these and other critical
components and assemble watches, television sets, and video
games.

The NICs' dilemma is that, in order to increase the value-added components, they have to expand to upstream products—like components and devices—or to the downstream operations—like marketing and distribution of their own branded goods. Both of these moves have proven to be extremely hard.

First, establishing the upstream business requires a lot of management resources, especially capital and engineering power. Take microchips, for example. One of its upstream businesses is the silicon single-crystal process, which is such a tough industry that there are only a half-dozen effective survivors in the entire Triad. Another element there is the "clean room," typically costing $100 million or more and requiring a very disciplined and skilled work force in order to achieve a yield high enough to be competitive.

Korea and Taiwan, with their leading-edge companies' capital formation and excellent educational system, are now beginning to enter these markets. However, even though they may accomplish the entry, the more profitable segments, such as high-speed 64K and 256K memory chips, charged couple devices, and gallium–arsenide semiconductors are still far away, at least on their own. Thus, it is a constant catch-up game. And in the process, if they are not very careful, these countries could end up producing only "engineered commodities," whose profit potential is marginal at best.

The second challenge for these countries is to move downstream. However, profitable downstream business means establishing a premium brand with your own distribution. Who has heard of any brand name goods from NICs? Despite their all-out efforts, perhaps the best known own brands so far are only Bata (shoes produced in India), Selangor (pewter made in Malaysia), and Samsung and Tatung (consumer electronics from Korea and Taiwan, respectively).

The reason you don't hear about them, despite their "dynamic growth" stories, is because the NICs are still, to a large extent, exporters of components and, subassemblies for other manufacturers. They produce goods to the specification of Triad nations' brand name manufacturers and distributors. Few of these Third World manufacturers even know about

156

the Triad customers' needs and desires directly. Thus, they lack the product design capability to develop a unique and appealing product, and they are hardly able to claim a premium price. These products therefore, are positioned as "low-end" or "price line" goods in the Triad's mass merchandising channels.

On top of the inherent low price nature of products produced in NICs, the Triad "downstreamers" take a very large margin of the profit. For example, in color television (or any other similar product, for that matter), a typical factory shipment price—hence, the amount of money the NIC companies receive—is anywhere between 15 and 25 percent of the list price in the Triad market. So, unless these new producers can establish their own distribution network for their own brand, there is very small profit potential left for them in the current business scheme of things.

In addition, an "own brand" strategy is not only expensive but also risky. Establishing a brand like Panasonic or Sony is a multi-billion-dollar project in the United States alone. Other brands, such as Toshiba, Sanyo, Sharp, Hitachi, MGA, TEAC, Akai, Epson, Pioneer, Sansui, Seiko, and Casio, have all spent over one hundred million dollars on the media and on dealers' cooperative programs to promote their brand. In fact, in most consumer products businesses, establishing their brand name in the Triad countries is far more expensive than building the production plant to make the product. One rule of thumb I have come up with from my own experience of working with Japanese companies is this: in order to establish the threshold awareness necessary to participate effectively in the global brand name race throughout the Triad regions, you need to invest $100 million and five years. Of course, this is the minimum, and if a company tries to spend anything below this, it might as well remain a supplier to original equipment manufacturers.

Very few companies in NICs have the capital and human resources to make that investment in either time or money to take over more value-added segments of the business system. Tatung (Taiwan) won an award at the 1982 Chicago Con-

157

sumer Electronics Show for its stereophonic products, a significant and perhaps epoch-marking event. In Korea, similar efforts are being pursued by their top companies such as Hyndai, Lucky, and Samsung. In a way, these Korean conglomerates have already become global in such businesses as ship building and plant construction in the developing regions by taking advantage of their lower cost and highly dedicated skilled workers. These are very good niches for them, in that they can be the lowest-cost provider of these kinds of products and services in the world, without having to invest in their own brands and distribution in the developed countries. And there is no expensive mass marketing involved.

But the long-term dilemma here is that it will be very difficult for NICs to use this route to increase their standard of living to the Triad's average because most companies in NICs are still buying blueprints and working on licenses from the Triad's technological giants rather than becoming the primary general contractors in macroprojects which produce, for example, high value-added plants. Until they make strategic investments they will be unable to claim higher prices. Should they all eventually approach the level of technological and marketing astuteness of the Triad regions, then their final challenge would still remain that of developing a large and hungry domestic market. Today's winning Triad nations depend to a large extent on their domestic markets rather than their exports. Japan's exports are responsible for only 13.3 percent of its GNP, despite its high rank among exporting nations. The United States has a large domestic market and only 8 percent of its GNP is exported. West Germany, Italy, the United Kingdom, and France are similar in this respect and export only 26, 22, 20, and 18 percent of their respective GNPs. These countries have a population in excess of 50 million each, with a GNP per capita of $10,000, except for Italy's $6,000. A typical worker earns anywhere between $10,000 in France to $18,000 in Japan.

In this context, only Korea has the potential of creating a sizable domestic market in this century, with its population of approximately 40 million. Taiwan has a population of 18 million, Hong Kong 5 million, and Singapore only 2.5 million. Korea's per capita GNP, however, was only one fifth that of Japan at $1,720 in 1981. Thus, with Japan growing at 4 percent per annum in real terms, Korea needs to grow steadily at 15 percent in real terms for the remainder of this century to gain the same per capita GNP as Japan. Even after that, the population difference would remain, resulting in Korea having only one third of Japan's domestic market in the year 2000.

Other countries, therefore, must try completely different national development strategies than "following Japan" and/or "catching up with the West," frequently used phrases in these countries. If Taiwan increased its GNP to $120 billion (its current GNP is $45 billion) that would put it on a par with Japan in terms of per capita GNP. That's equivalent to only two General Motors, or three IBMs, or five General Electrics, including their sphere of influence over subcontractors and vendors to make the comparison apple-to-apple. If Singapore's GNP doubled to $25 billion, it would be on a par with the Triad's per capita GNP. That, again, is equivalent to only one and a half Nissans or Toyotas, three Hondas, or five Kobe Steel. In other words, instead of diffusing their resources in many industries, the NICs really need to concentrate on a few favorite industries to become truly global. Then, these countries could support their populations and give their people a standard of living comparable to Triad residents.

However, this is not what the NICs are doing. They are spreading their resources thinly and confusing their own citizens as well as foreign investors. For example, they want to build chemical refineries, steel plants, electronics plants, computers, medicines, cars, textiles, and telecommunications, all at the same time as they are building highways and subways, as well as running a national flag carrier airline and an army, navy, and air force.

In order to achieve these goals quickly, they want to attract foreign capital. Thus they build tax-free zones where foreign companies can produce. From the viewpoint of the host country, these companies in the tax-free zones are not fully participating in the national economy, but are simply using labor at marginal costs. Tax-free zones seldom help to build the national economy, in terms of value-added increments, taxes and technology transfer. When times get bad, these foreign producers will migrate farther to the south, and what is left behind is higher wage rates and unemployment. Tax-free zones should be a means of developing the nation and not an end in themselves. Unless the nation has clear long-term strategies as to what to do with its own people, these short-term relief measures do not become a solution.

It is amazing to find that very few of these countries, the NICs and the LDCs alike, have a clear industrial policy setting forth their industrial development priorities. They have to realize that even with the best strategies and with the fullest degree of implementation, their probability of success is rather poor. This is all the more likely when they do not have a set of special priorities setting guidelines and a full commitment to execution.

Key Points for Developing Countries

Although the specific solution is different from country to country, based on my personal experience of working as an industrial policy adviser to some of these countries, I can certainly point out the following general directions for these countries:

1. Emphasize education above all, but do not treat the educated as a special privileged group. Teach them to become leaders rather than elites.

2. Select only several priority industries with which to establish global preeminence. Build the entire supporting infrastructure sequentially over time, encompassing both downstream and upstream operations.

3. Separate import-substituting industries from export-building ones, and do not regulate the latter in the same way as the former.

160

4. Remove complex licensing processes and regulations on industries because these tend not only to stifle entrepreneurship, but also to become sources of corruption.

5. Use taxpayers' money for building a national infrastructure for industrialization, such as providing low-cost commodities and raw materials, utilities, communications, and transportation. Conversely, leave the development of the industrial sector to private enterprise.

6. Encourage indigenous entrepreneurs, because the long-term health of a nation's economy really depends on its people's ability to reinvest for growth in their own country.

7. Encourage foreign investors to come in as "full citizens," i.e., to establish complete business systems rather than only assembly or distribution units. This means you have to give them relatively unregulated access to the local market. In return you can expect them to build state-of-the-art operations, whose profit can be taxed *after* they establish world-class competitiveness.

8. Continue to communicate with your people about their views of the government and their aspirations for the nation. Demonstrate every few years how much progress has been made, and draw up a new national agenda.

Obviously, these guidelines have been heavily influenced by my upbringing in Japan, and by my having studied the Japanese government's almost artistic strategies for molding 100 million people into a leading industrial nation. However, I have to say that the principles of strategy, in a tough, competitive world, ought not to be treated lightly. The world does consist of 150 nations participating in a competitive marketplace. Unless a nation has a sellable product, no one has to buy. In fact, they don't. No matter what artificial incentives one government might set up, they will not make sense over

161

time and/or with respect to the other things the government must do. The world economy, in gross terms, is governed by the principles of survival of the fittest. While the United Nations Conference on Trade and Development, ASEAN, the EC, OPEC, and other forms of transnational consortia have been formed to take advantage of a particular set of commonalities of nations' interests, they have clearly failed to act as a fraternal commune.

In NICs and LDCs, the government tends to be highly visible and run by an elite. They are better versed and informed than the general public. Bureaucrats participate in United Nations meetings and all kinds of international organizations and conferences. As a result, they tend to build their country for the sake of it. They might build harbors without supporting industries and their infrastructure. They might build the highways and railways to an extent that is three decades ahead of the current need for them given the amount of traffic.

Now, why do we need to worry about NICs and LDCs in discussing Triad power? Throughout this book, I have laid out the currents of change taking place in the Triad nations and the need for global corporations to form consortia to penetrate deeper into the more critical markets of the world. This is the survival plan for Triad corporations. They do not have the luxury of escaping from these realities. This, in turn, will create a greater gap in wealth-generating capabilities between the Triad, and the NIC and the LDCs.

In this chapter, I have tried to diagnose the causes of this gap and to suggest that these developing countries use more of a free enterprise model in their policy formulation, rather than the heavy—and frankly outmoded—governmental control model. Very few of these countries have a GNP greater than 50 billion dollars. So it shouldn't be too difficult for them to treat themselves as a global-scale company, rather than simply as an isolated nation controlled by a government; at least this will serve to generate new perspectives and alternatives to the conventional wisdom of government control. This will certainly stimulate national debate, and the net result will be a much more dynamic and realistic outlook.

Now, then, where do the Triad's global corporations fit in this scheme? And how should they treat these developing regions? You have probably guessed by now that I would very much like to encourage any Triad company to treat a few of these countries as equal partners to form a global consortium. No company can learn enough about 150 countries to enable it to make money in each of them. Each country is different.

So I would ask Triad firms: why not choose a few developing nations and get to know them very well? Once you do, then think about building a global-scale operation taking advantage of your in-depth knowledge of one or several select countries, your relationships with its people, and the relative cost advantage of the chosen host countries. Be prepared to contribute to the attainment of the nations' goals, as you would undoubtedly do for your own home country. Clearly distinguish these operations from opportunistic, small-scale plants built to enter each of the restricted markets. Around these strong operations in the chosen countries, you should expect to build—over time—a great number of interrelationships with the neighboring countries for raw materials and component supplies, as well as marketing and distribution.

Going one step farther, you can use the key country operation as a training ground for management talents. For example, the key languages in Latin America are Portuguese and Spanish. Managers, once trained, could be transferred across national boundaries (but within the region) much more successfully than shifting U.S. managers fresh from the States into these countries all the time.

Likewise, in Southeast Asia, the key languages are Chinese and Malay. A Chinese manager fully trained in Taiwan can be moved to Hong Kong, Singapore, and to some extent to other business communities with high Overseas Chinese populations, such as Malaysia, Indonesia, and Thailand. While each country has a different culture, national flavor, and self-identity, moving managers within the region makes much more sense than transferring Japanese managers back and forth across the national boundaries. The same analogy applies to the Arabic nations and some parts of Africa.

163

In the Tetrahedon model of the Triad, an extension of the basic Triad concept, the "As" (for Asia) in the diagram in Exhibit IV–1 is not intended to represent a static Asia which is purely a geographic area. Rather, "As" stands for a number of countries, each with the potential to be internalized and tailormade. A Triad Power must invest to establish linkages with, and make commitments to, the region. This, in my view, is the only way global corporations in this region could act as meaningful world citizens who want to help solve the otherwise unmanageable problems between the northern and southern countries. Multinational enterprises in the 1960s and 1970s created rather negative images of selfishness, exploitation, and self-governance. That kind of image is not good for the home country, nor for the host countries. In the future, Triad companies participating in the developing world can act as much more sensible, responsible, and meaningful enterprises. It is a unique opportunity for them, and the task should not be left to political governments, which are already malfunctioning and have a tendency to get involved in unrealistic diplomatic exercises.

11

MERITS OF BEING A TRIAD POWER

MY BASIC OBSERVATION is that, as a company has (1) equal penetration and exploitation capabilities, and (2) no blind spots in each of the Triad regions, it can become an effective Triad power. The first condition is necessary in order to recover the firm's investment on its unique and diversified products. The second condition is necessary because such a firm wants to avoid surprises from foreign competitors or domestic competitors forming alliances with foreign companies.

These are the defensive reasons why a company wants to satisfy the two conditions above. Because if it doesn't, it is likely to fall into a vicious cycle of decline. Why the motorcycle, camera, and watch industries in the United States and Europe failed is completely beyond me.

The Japanese once occupied Singapore after traveling down the Malay Peninsula on bicycles. The British armed forces lost their morale and fighting spirit, it is said, because they were frightened by rumors that a merciless Japanese Imperial Army was marching down to take over Singapore. They did not remember Sun Tzu's famous teaching: Know thy enemy, and thyself, and thou shalt win one hundred battles.

Talking to the Japanese executives who have fought the wars in these industries (e.g., motorcycles, cameras, and watches), one amazingly common comment emerges: they never thought the fighting would be so easy. They were expecting retaliation, tough negotiation, Machiavellian division of the Japanese competitors themselves, and in the end a superb and low-cost product to wipe out the Japanese, who, after all, have less experience in industry and in doing business around the world.

Instead, what happened? In the motorcycle industry, for instance, Honda came up with a really tiny bike, a 50-cc model with a high-speed engine and a competitive cost. Most European and American manufacturers, meanwhile, were moving up from medium- to high-class vehicles. Their stated reason was, "We can't compete with these guys who pay one tenth the wages!"

So when Honda made money in the low end, Yamaha and Suzuki joined the bandwagon to take the joy ride. With the money they made, they moved up to the 125- and 250-cc class, which in the mid-1960s in Japan was the super high end of the product line. Honda's ad campaign said, "You meet beautiful people on a Honda," to erase the Hell's Angels image of bikers, and American and European consumers became Honda's "beautiful customers."

Honda, at that time, was nothing but a vendor of auto components for Toyota. The firm had no money and no people to speak of. The only difference between Honda and the established American and European motorcycle producers was Soichiro Honda himself.

Michiaki Nishida, the former executive vice-president and a lifetime collaborator of Soichiro Honda, once told me that, when he joined the company 35 years ago, it was a small automobile repair company with only 50 employees. But Soichiro Honda gave a pep talk every morning, standing on a tangerine box and telling his employees, "We will become global. We've got to become global. We have to get out of this [humiliating] subcontractor situation!" So American and European producers abandoned medium-sized motorcycles

166

to concentrate on "high-value-added" vehicles, high-class motorcycles with 500- and 750-cc engines. With the huge investment in production technology and the basic R&D required to become a global supplier of the low- and medium-class of the mass markets, Honda and other joyriders actually transformed themselves into modern technology-driven companies.

At any time during the 20-year span between 1955 and 1975, any serious study would have enabled leading American and European motorcycle producers to either retaliate head-to-head or to form alliances with either Suzuki or Kawasaki. Suzuki later tied up with General Motors (GM) in the passenger car industry, and Kawasaki Heavy Industries (KHI) has a history of alliances and licensing agreements with Western companies across their product line, from aircraft to robots. It is well known that its licensing agreement with Unimation in Japan made KHI the leading spot welding robot producer in the world. It is a company that knows both Eastern and Western markets.

Despite these possibilities, none of the Western companies really did anything with these available strategic options. Instead, they considered the whole Japanese move as a "threat," "unfair," and a "peril." And top executives of the Western corporations lobbied politically to set quotas and tariffs.

In Japan alone, there were as many as 204 motorcycle producers in the 1950s. Only four companies have survived. It wasn't an easy race for the Japanese, either. But the surviving companies were really tough and resilient. Before crying out for political asylum, European and U.S. motorcycle companies should have really studied the key factors for survival.

In the field of cameras, the situation was very similar. The fact that Japan has over a dozen internationally known camera companies—Nikon, Canon, Konica, Minolta, Olympus, Fujica, Yashica, Mamiya, and Topcon, among others—does not mean that anybody in Japan can produce a good camera. In fact, most of these companies do nothing but design the basic camera mechanism. They purchase lenses, shutter mech-

167

anisms, and camera bodies, and in only a few cases do they manufacture all the parts for a complete camera.

Of course, the top-tier companies polish their own lenses and manufacture critical components. But the vendors of components, who are willing to sell to anybody in the world, are equally competent. So there were ample opportunities in the 1960s and early 1970s for European and American companies to either import critical components from Japan and produce the same quality camera as the Japanese were making, or to establish a production base in Japan to take advantage of the Japanese component suppliers' infrastructure and become an "honorary Japanese" camera company distributing their products under the Western brand name through their distribution network in the United States and Europe.

During the same time period, IBM and Texas Instruments were building plants in Japan, and most German chemical conglomerates were expanding their Japanese base rapidly. There was no rational reason why the German camera companies had to fight the Japanese in Germany, though, in the end, one of them ended up in Singapore, which is absolutely the wrong place to fight the Japanese top manufacturers. Nor was there any reason why companies like Polaroid with its instant camera or Kodak with its 110 Pocket Camera could not have bought a Japanese single-lens reflex camera company or established one on its own and thereby expanded their camera range from the instant and low end all the way to lens–shutter and single-lens reflex products.

The Westerners had plenty of opportunities. At least a half-dozen Japanese camera companies were being wiped out by Canon's dominance, and they were completely out of breath. Ailing Yashica was bought in 1983 by Kyocera, a ceramics company. And Mamiya was bought by a venture capital group named Cosmo 80, a total misfit to begin with. A more natural fit would have been for Western establishments to establish a foothold in the Japanese precision machining and mechatronics (the combination of mechanics and electronics) industries by acquiring one of these Japanese camera companies or their manufacturing subsidiaries.

All in all, in the industries where Western companies abandoned the market to the Japanese companies—similar to the British capitulation in Singapore—it is clear that the European and American companies really did not have insider knowledge about the Japanese. Perhaps this is because they didn't have the confidence that they could fight back effectively, counter the threats to their positions, or deal with the risks of buying into the weaker members of the seemingly indistinguishable group (from Western eyes) of Japanese competitors. As a result, the Western companies fell into a vicious cycle: giving up their main segments, concentrating on relatively peaceful niches, confining their activities to the domestic market, and repeating the "cost reduction and removal of overhead" cycle. In the end, they became insignificant contenders in the mainstream of the global marketplace.

The most significant advantage of becoming a Triad power is not only to stop this regrettable vicious circle, but also to enable a corporation to form a positive and more offensive strategy. Knowing the basic desires of the 600 million inhabitants of the Triad, the company can come up with a universal product. Or, having come up with a very competitive product at home, it can tailor frills and looks to local tastes. And, it can market simultaneously to 600 million people.

With mighty sales forces in each of the three Triad regions, either their own or a partners', companies can strike into the market in a relatively short time and preempt the opportunities of both local and global competitors. Thus they can rake in a lot of money, resulting in a high return on their initial investment. With this profit, they can reinvest in more sophisticated and complex facilities and/or R&D, to pose a real challenge to the local companies or to a half-baked, crippled Triad company. Should any local company come up with a mighty new product, the Triad power can copy it, and cleverly preempt its opportunities in the other two Triad markets. With the profit generated there, the Triad power can comfortably fight a head-to-head battle with the originating company on its own turf. For example, Schick's alliance with Seiko has given it such distribution power in Japan that the Gillette double-blade razor is better known by the Japanese as Schick Super II.

The company that invented the product, having lost profit opportunities, must generate funds to fight against the Triad power, using the precious little profit it has derived from its home country which, in the end, is hardly enough to recover its inventing and launching costs.

The merits of being acquainted with the 600 million people in the Triad regions and all of the key competitors therein are so clear that the issue is not *whether* a company should become a Triad power but rather *how* it should do so. Therefore, I urge that readers move right into the following "how-to" section next.

THE ROAD TO BECOMING
A TRIAD POWER

THE CRITICAL IMPORTANCE of being an insider needs no further elaboration. It is sufficient to say that judging and responding to competition, technology, and customer trends from a great distance is at best unsatisfactory and at worst unworkable. In this last chapter, let us consider how your company can become a true Triad power by examining alternative routes, structures, and value systems.

Alternative Routes

There are three basic ways to becoming an effective insider, each not exclusive of the others. They can be taken in order of equity integration:

Consortia

As we saw in Chapter 9, there are many examples of emerging loose consortia in key industries, such as automobiles and semiconductors. The purpose is to seek partners in other Triad regions to supplement functional shortcomings in order to survive and even expand in home regions. These consortia are formed to share or trade certain upstream functions such as R&D, production, and technology, and to stay abreast of the leading-edge companies; consortia seldom include a full range of manufacturing and sales and marketing activities. Sometimes, consortia involve swapping certain product categories in order to take advantage of synergies made possible by sharing critical functions, but rarely does a partner give up an entire function.

Despite the journalistic emphasis on "trade war" stories, this form of cooperation is becoming increasingly popular in industries that have been widely publicized as "antagonistic." Recently, an executive vice-president of a large U.S. chemical company visited half a dozen Japanese chemical companies to seek areas of mutual synergy. To his surprise, more than three companies expressed a strong interest in sharing various resources. Frequently we have been involved in transregional discussions involving automobiles, large-scale integrated circuits, pharmaceuticals, communications, computers, and other areas. There is a clear indication today that the top management of global enterprises are seriously interested in protecting home market positions, and if necessary, are willing to cooperate with other Triad-region competitors rather than fight them off in destructive trade wars. This reflects a change in their perspective on competition and global business. In other words, we have entered an era of global competition between the most powerful survivors, regardless of origin. Because of the universality of user needs, because of the expensive development costs, and because of the number of companies seeking large-scale production automation, many companies that rely solely on their home markets now find their strategies obsolete.

However, forming consortia does not mean that all companies should invest indiscriminately in all regions of their key markets to produce and sell their products. For one thing, companies have to consider with whom they should seek consortia links. Two bases for a decision are geography and industry. Consortia allies should not be too close or in your own Triad region. Distant foes can be real friends, while close cousins can be foes (Exhibit 12–1). You can see this in the European transnational mergers. Most of those mergers failed because they involved links between similar companies, which ended up by hating each other. They could not work as partners because they were too close, and their businesses were too much alike.

Fundamentally, companies thinking about forming consortia should try to objectively reassess their implicit strategy. The most useful ground rule, then, is to maximize the contribution to critical fixed costs. If R&D becomes expensive, make sure the resultant product is sold all over the world, regardless of your existing (spotty) selling capabilities in certain regions. If your production facility is at the state-of-the-art stage and very expensive, but could operate at a low cost if fully utilized, then you should think about selling your products to any firm with strong distribution capabilities, to original equipment manufacturers, or under your own brand name.

If you have a mighty sales force and/or distribution channel, but your laboratory cannot pump out enough new products, then think about importing other companies' strong

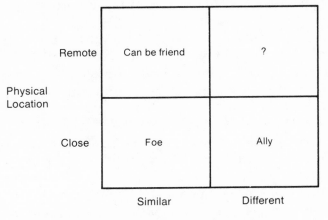

EXHIBIT 12–1 Consortia/syndication.

products. If you remember the fact that most product lines acquire a larger value-added increment during distribution, rather than in production, this kind of choice is not too far out of alignment from sensible and contemporary strategic thinking.

A proven product from outside is probably a better bet than a series of unproven home-grown, new products. This, of course, does not mean that I am encouraging everyone to become a distributor. My point is simply that one should remain objective about the profit-contribution potential of any product line one hopes to internalize.

All of these measures, whether they leverage R&D, manufacturing, or distribution, are based on the concept of maximizing the product's contribution to fixed costs. At a very high level of abstraction, my Triad consortia proposal is based on this pragmatic doctrine of management wisdom.

The secret is simply that you expand your sphere of imagination to the globe in applying the doctrine. Enlarge your search for sources and potential contributors outside traditional neighborhood "shopping areas," and go global for the hunt. If your rivals are doing so, then your only option is to do so better. And that is the reason why I say the global competition will not only become a battle among the most powerful companies, but also among the most powerful consortia as allies.

The organizational implications of international consortia are psychologically complex. Consortia and collaborative arrangements with traditional competitors are seldom welcomed by middle managers whose interest is to show top management that they are as capable as anybody else. Some essential programs for the success of a consortium include carrying out a good internal communications campaign to explain the intent of the consortium, building multitier relationships among the companies forming the consortium, and positioning the liaison office at the top. Too many consortia have come into being with enormous enthusiasm at the onset, only to fade away subsequently because there were no managed and systematic efforts to maintain that enthusiasm.

A corporation tends to forgive its own internal mistakes, but has a terrible habit of accusing—and being visibly disappointed by—its partner's mistakes. Since consortia formation is a product of convenience and/or strategic importance, a diplomatic maturing is needed to sustain constructive intercompany relationships.

Joint Ventures

A joint venture across the Triad regions is a formal and legal recognition of a cooperative consortium relationship. Philips has a long and successful history of joint ventures with Matsushita in electronic components. Similarly, though its share has been slipping, Caterpillar's joint venture with Mitsubishi Heavy Industries has given it staying power in the rather conservative earth-moving equipment market of Japan. High Voltage Industries (HVI), a 50–50 joint venture between GE and Hitachi in gas switch gear in Philadelphia, uses GE's mighty pooled sales force for utility customers and Hitachi's advanced SF6 gas diffusion technology.

By and large, joint ventures are normally designed to take advantage of the strong functions of partners and supplement the weak functions—be it management, resources, or marketing—of one's own company. The recent announcement of a joint venture plan in small business computers between Matsushita and IBM is a good example of resource sharing with each company supplementing each other's functional strengths. This joint venture also conveys the fact that even the biggest companies in two regions of the Triad cannot single-handedly fight and win the electronics war.

Too often, however, joint ventures fail. One major deterrent to success is that joint ventures are legal entities with equity sharing. Disputes over investments or resource allocation can be frequent and can frustrate joint venture goals. Unlike loosely coupled consortia, joint ventures must decide how to split profit (or loss) and where and how to reinvest for the future. This requires that the management philosophy

175

of the two (or more) companies forming a joint venture must be similar and compatible. It is reported that Nihon Seiko Kabushiki Kaisha (NSK), a leading Japanese ball bearing company, bought a 50 percent equity share of its 50–50 joint venture, Hoover–NSK Bearing, from Hoover Ball and Bearing to set up its own 100 percent subsidiary. The reason given was differences in investment attitude; NSK claimed Hoover was reluctant to invest aggressively during the depression of the mid-1970s.

Likewise, Toshiba dissolved its 50–50 color television production joint venture with Rank in the United Kingdom, and had to go it alone to turn the situation around. Since Rank has participated in a joint venture with Xerox in Europe, it should have the experience to be a successful partner with other companies. On the other hand, Rank may have had too strong a stereotypic (and successful) image of how a "marriage" should work, which Toshiba might have found a hard act to follow. The most likely explanation, however, is that neither party was prepared to go through the agonies of giving birth to a new baby.

Other companies have shown more determination. When Matsushita went to Cardiff (Wales) to build color televisions, their vendors did not follow delivery schedules and, when deliveries were made, the parts had over 30 percent reject rates for most critical components. British television set makers did not seem to mind this quality problem too much, and shipped rather incomplete products to the market. Customers' defense against this was not to buy a set, but to lease one; if it broke, the leasing company would repair it. The country's infrastructure was built to make up for the shortcomings of the component industry. It took companies like Matsushita and Sony ten years working with their vendors to reduce the reject rate to below 1 percent. Although this was still ten times higher than that in Japan, it was certainly at a workable level. These companies had to grit their teeth through the birth pains and suffer unpredictable operations in order to survive in Europe.

A joint venture, or a multiple of companies, does not normally possess these traits. It is a combination of da Vinci's brain and Carl Lewis's legs. When one wants to fly, the other might insist on running. And frequently, both are right. Thus, what is required at the onset is the understanding by both parties involved that in order to make a joint venture a success, it takes as much effort as building a new greenfield plant. The understanding has to include a priori which party will take care of which pains and agonies.

Setsutaro Kobayashi, founder of Fuji Film, states in his autobiography[1] that he wanted to join hands with Xerox. He could see the day of dry copy on plain paper coming, and this would affect his silver bromide-based film business. He wanted to form a joint venture in the field of xerography as if he'd wanted to give birth to his own child. So subsequently, when the 50–50 joint venture negotiation was consummated, he sent his son, Yotaro (Tony), to manage the company. Even after Setsutaro's untimely death in 1977, Tony never came back to Fuji Film to succeed his father as CEO, but remained at Fuji–Xerox, and made it a highly reputable $1 billion enterprise in Japan's fiercely competitive office automation industry.

Another successful joint venture in Japan is Yamatake–Honeywell, in which Honeywell owns 50 percent, the Yasuda group about 16.5 percent, and the rest is in the form of stock available on the Tokyo Stock Exchange. Established in 1949, it has grown to be number two in the Japanese process control and instrumentation field, with an annual turnover of about $310 million. It has maintained very good relationships with both parents; Honeywell has been able to inject needed technologies, and the Japanese partner has supplied a stable management team.

A joint venture is like marriage. It takes a great amount of effort on the part of both parties in order to make it a success over a prolonged time that may include different environments, relative strengths, and varying aspirations. The relationship never stays the same as it was when the contract was first drawn up.

Unlike a marriage, a joint venture unfortunately has nu-

177

merous legal contracts and forms of capital participation. There is not, therefore, the flexibility of talking out frustrations aloud to thrash out differences. People normally run to legal contracts to point out the partner's violations. Even if operating division managers didn't do so, legal advisors would. In order to "gain control," one partner often wants to decrease the other's equity share. If you think you can control emotions, will, and enthusiasm for success by controlling equity, you are wrong. Emotions can never be bought with a "controlling majority."

It is my experience that majority voting seldom represents good business judgment and seldom favors entrepreneurial decisions. However, by definition, joint ventures tend to *vote* on critical matters in proportion to the equity holding. Partners make a mistake in the joint venture if they give too much weight to money, i.e., equity. You can pretty safely conclude that, if a voting process is needed to decide on critical matters, the joint venture has already failed. Likewise, if you need the world's best lawyers to spell out all possible details and countermeasures against potential disputes, you as a company do not have a good basis for the corporate marriage known as a joint venture.

1. Make sure on both sides of the venture that there is at least one sponsor, and that each one has the firm conviction that the joint venture is good for the company and is a meaningful undertaking.

2. Keep sponsors responsible for the joint venture for a long time, say, at least a decade or two.

3. Have active cross-breeding and frequent mutual face-to-face communications at least at three layers of the organization, that is, top management, operational leaders, and work force.

4. Above all, communicate rather than control.

These are all human factors. It is important to realize that, although contracts are exchanged between the two companies, the actual work has to be carried out by people. So, in spelling out the dynamics, think as if you are writing the contract for yourself, or for your family. An "institution" is an abstract noun, and is of no use in reality, especially at times of trouble.

The above four points represent only the minimum conditions necessary from my personal experience and certainly do not represent sufficient conditions to succeed, for example, superior production technology, cost, strategy, product competitiveness, and the like. Nonetheless, it is amazing to find how many joint ventures don't even actually satisfy these four basic conditions.

Through my many observations of these corporate relationships, I have come to realize that corporations actually have a blood type. One company may have blood type A, and the other type B. If you make a forced transfusion, both parties pass out. Some companies speak only in financial terms, while others talk technology. Some companies love to develop a detailed business plan, while others—though equally excellent—don't even have a formal planning process.

These differences eventually form what is known as corporate culture or corporate personality. It is sometimes sublimated into the particular "language" a corporation uses. Different corporations with different languages cannot talk to each other. It doesn't matter what they are talking about. Even within the same country, two corporations have totally different personalities and resultant "languages." Daiichi Kangyo Bank is Japan's biggest city bank, formed in 1970 as a merger between Daiichi Bank (D) and Kangyo (K) Bank. Today, 15 years after the merger, they are still fighting over every question possible and taking turns between the ex-D and ex-K members for a given position.

On the other hand, we hear about Ciba-Geigy and Nippon Steel as if they were a single company to begin with. These are examples of the "perfect marriages." But behind these perfect marriages, I know there has been a lot of good judgment, sound decisions, and fair rules.

When more than one company is involved, there is no

179

"natural" fit. There has to be extremely careful planning, and a lot of giving, before starting to think about harvesting the joint fruits. Joint ventures are the same as farming in this context.

On the more mundane organizational and operational side, a joint venture must be clearly positioned relative to existing divisions. Many joint ventures are formed by a handful of top executives and staff members, and their position in relation to the existing corporate functions and operating divisions is often unclear. Without full cooperation or resource reallocation, the joint venture becomes a "stepchild." Therefore, prior to forming a joint venture, it is of key importance to spend sufficient time with those who will be *operationally involved* once the joint venture is set into motion.

Wholly Owned Company

This is the traditional model of a multinational enterprise and needs no detailed discussion. However, three points for successful implementation should be mentioned.

1. Establish a "regional" structure rather than a country-level focus to share common resources.

2. Shift the role of headquarters from that of a controller to a strategic lubricator across key regions of the Triad.

3. Give equal "citizenship" to four key areas, as in the Tetrahedron model.

Compare, for example, the traditional multinational organizational structure with that of the German chemical giant BASF, which reorganized in 1981. It still preserves the regional grouping of its nonstrategic areas, but treats the key strategic countries completely separately. Therefore, the heads of BASF's U.S., Japanese, and Brazilian subsidiaries—the last region represents an important "hinterland" to BASF—each report directly to a director who is a member

180

of the BASF executive board. Tailor-made policies for each of the three areas continues to be worked out. This kind of organization is a realistic solution to the problem of organizing any multinational enterprise.

Too many multinationals put Japan in the Far East Department or the Pacific Basin Division of the International Business Sector. This means that the head of the Japanese operations, despite that country's critical strategic difference from other Asian countries, is positioned five layers below the CEO. We have seen many instances where the head of a multinational corporation's (MNC) Japanese operation is positioned below a sales manager in Denver. Similarly, we have seen many Japanese companies send a deputy general manager from production planning to the United States to head up their U.S. operations. This is the quickest way to undermine operations in the Triad region.

Alternative Structures

Headquarters' role should be defined by the synergy it can provide to keep its key operating units flexible and responsive to the marketplace. The scope of this role is defined by finding out where the most value-added increment can be brought about by the corporate functions. As a corporation develops its presence in each key Triad region, the regional headquarters will gradually take on the traditional home country headquarter's control and will offer lower-cost service functions to various country subsidiaries by pooling capabilities to get better functional synergies.

In this context, it is very useful to think about three alternative forms of governing different regions and countries.

The Multinational Corporation

The multinational corporation is the traditional form, where headquarters has the dominant role and does all the planning and control. Resources are allocated according to the business plan, and most frequently preference is given to the domestic market and large operations, regardless of the strategic importance of the region. For example, if the Thai operation happens to be big for some historical coincidence, then good talent is shipped in and higher priorities are given. In other words, most interactions take the form of local subsidiary versus headquarters, and there is very little regional and/or transnational synergy. This focus on headquarters tends to give it excessive power, and headquarters, in turn, starts viewing the world from the red carpet of Park Avenue, Marunouchi, or St. James's Street.

Another opposite but extreme case is to treat all countries in the same way, and that is the "United Nations syndrome." This approach, of course, appears very democratic, but it tends to do better, as we have seen, in smaller and less competitive countries. However, it tends to create problems in tough and large markets in the Triad. The local operation of most MNCs tend to be shallow in terms of their ability to respond to differences in country markets, and the value system of corporate headquarters tends to prevail over the management in the particular country.

Multilocal Company

A successful MNC frequently is actually an assembly of excellent local companies with strong local autonomy. Coca-Cola is a good example of a company made up of many successful local companies, as a result of a very clever strategy of inviting local capital to establish route sales and bottlers' networks in each country entered. Each country, therefore, is unique in terms of management talents and capital, but throughout the world the company has the same successful recipe of merchandising and distribution strategies.

Multilocal companies (MLCs) constitute a very effective approach in that they accomplish a true insiderization with indigenous management teams for a given country. If your company is blessed with unique talents, then you must encourage the local entrepreneurs to the extent that the resultant company is significantly different in terms of its practices of hiring, promotion, and in the way it relates to the local community. In an extreme situation, product development could be carried out uniquely and autonomously by each country's management.

"When in Rome, do as the Romans do" is the modus operandi of the MLC. As a result, the probability of success is quite high if the company has a basically sound product–market concept, and headquarters remains resourceful and flexible, as opposed to being dogmatic and partial.

However, one of the shortcomings of the MLC is the lack of emphasis on certain key countries and regions, as well as forceful and strategic interlinkages to extract synergy from a global and/or regional operation.

Local autonomy often gets in the way of healthy coordination by the regional and/or headquarters' staff to ensure competitive advantages over (1) local and provincial companies, and (2) simplistic and monolithic global operators. Local autonomy, unless supplemented by a broader perspective, can ultimately result in a few blind spots when serious competitive erosions are taking place in critical countries. "By-the-bottom-line" country managers tend to delay the bad news, or when it is conveyed, headquarters' executives often disregard such signals as "special aberrations."

Economically, an MLC could be reinventing the wheel in each country, in terms of possessing a full set of the functions in the business system. Such functions as R&D, legal, personnel development, branding, and manufacturing could be shared among multiple countries. This may result in higher costs due to the more expensive ways of doing the things typical of a foreign company, whereas a truly local company could do more cheaply with local wages and disciplines. On average, foreign companies operating in Japan pay some 20 percent higher wages in order to attract personnel to an enterprise perceived from overseas as "less permanent."

Japanese companies in the United States and Europe also

end up paying more in wages for lower-quality personnel than their indigenous contenders. These are the "antes" foreign companies must pay. If there were no areas to save money, elsewhere via synergistic savings by sharing some functional costs, for example, then a global enterprise wouldn't have any hope of cost advantage, and hence it would have to compete genuinely on new ideas and innovative concepts. As we have seen in Parts II and III, this is a rather unrealistic expectation, and should not be counted on a priori.

Multiregional Company

The Tetrahedron has four regions of strategic emphasis—the three Triad regions plus one developing region—along with dozens of other marginal countries outside of these regions. The next logical step of the MLC is the multiregional company (MRC), where it makes sense. You have simply bundled up the local operations and formed the regional headquarters to interact and communicate with other regions in the critical Tetrahedron regions.

The MRC can also be viewed as a natural step in the evolution in the multinational company in that the headquarters has become extremely sensitive about the commonalities of the regions and yet flexible about the uniqueness of the key marketplaces. As such, regional headquarters are formed in such a way as to complement each other across the Tetrahedron, and yet to facilitate global resource reallocation and utilization against key competitive threats. Common functions are shared in the regions and across the regions in such a way as to gain synergistic advantage over competitors' quality and cost position.

Since it helps to clarify many conceptual problems associated with the Triad, let me elaborate about the MRC, which is at least structurally closest to the Triad concept. Needless to say, one can operate a global enterprise on the Triad concept without taking the physical shape of the MRC. For example, you can tie up with someone in Europe and operate on your own only in Japan and the United States, and you can still maintain the Triad perspective at the corporate center.

Role of Regional Company

Because it is important to respond to consumers' needs and competitive moves at large, if a company operates as an MRC does not mean that regional headquarters should take over the roles uniquely played by local companies and/or global headquarters. Exhibit 12–2 illustrates the correct division of labor. What I want to emphasize is not the size of the shaded area which represents the relative importance of regional headquarters in each of the Tetrahedron regions.

Rather, my point in introducing this conceptual framework is to highlight the need to consider the different elements of the business system in determining the optimal balance of the division of responsibilities and roles among the three distinctively different levels of management in the structure of a global company. Some functions, such as sales and logistics, could be best performed autonomously by the country management. Manufacturing could be also left entirely to the local management if the cost of logistics and/or needs for localization are high, as is the case for consumer packaged goods, beverages, and cement. On the other hand, manufacturing could best be carried out regionally if economies of scale are critical and procurement is regional. Likewise, if a dominant competitor is a regional operator, then this competitor's effect on cost and the impact of a regional-scale plant—rather than local-scale plant—needs to be assessed.

Many Europeans use different brands in different countries. Very few Japanese consumer electronics companies do this. As a result of this implicit "pan-European" branding policy, Japanese companies are able to use relatively inexpensive—but effective for the high-class segment—advertising media, such as airline in-flight magazines and signboards near major airports and business commercial streets. For example, driving out of Schipol Airport in Holland makes me feel very

185

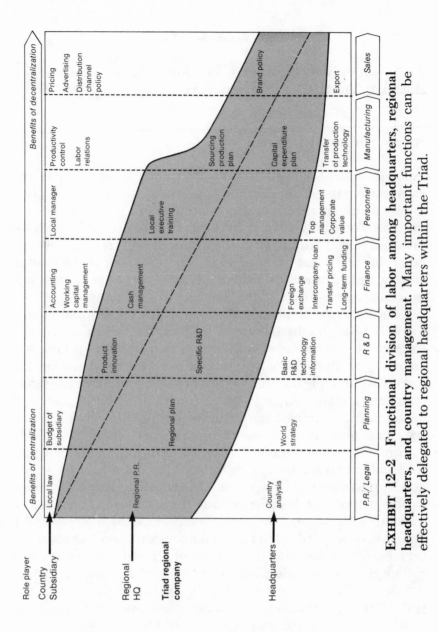

EXHIBIT 12–2 Functional division of labor among headquarters, regional headquarters, and country management. Many important functions can be effectively delegated to regional headquarters within the Triad.

much "at home" as I see billboards displaying Canon and Ricoh products all around me. Likewise, New York's Times Square and London's Piccadilly Circus are flooded with neon signs advertising Japanese consumer and office products with "pan-Triad" brands.

However, some Japanese companies have been stuck with numerous brands. For example, Matsushita Electric Industrial uses the National brand in Japan, Asia, and Europe, but due to a trademark registration conflict it could not use National in the United States. It ended up with "Panasonic," a slightly more ambitious name than "Sony." I personally believe it is a very good brand and certainly a highly prestigious one in North America. However, as a result of this, and as a result of its acquisition of Motorola's television division, it now has yet another brand, Quasar. On top of this, it introduced the Technics brand at the high end of its audiophonic line. So, compared with Sony, whose company name is the same as its brand name, Matsushita has ended up investing advertising money in Matsushita (for corporate identity), Panasonic (as a company, as well as one of the brands, in North America), Quasar (originally for both company and brand, now for brand only, in North America), National as a brand, and JVC through its subsidiary, named Japan Victor Company. JVC is a company established by RCA in Japan in 1927, but which was later acquired by Matsushita after its ownership shifted several times from RCA to Mitsubishi Nissan to Tokyo Denki to Industrial Bank of Japan. It is remarkable that, despite the natural disadvantages, Matsushita has done very well with its pan-regional branding strategies. But multibrand strategies are not recommended unless you are as powerful a giant as Matsushita or Unilever.

I can cite several functions which regional headquarters can fulfill well (Exhibit 12–2). One of them is personnel management, particularly management of the career path for talented people. Often global enterprises cannot recruit talented local workers. One of the biggest problems is the absence of upward potential for local workers in their careers. The office of head of the company in a country can belong to only one person. Other functions may not be challenging, given head-quarters' functional and operating divisions' strong controls.

So, unlike their local competitors, there are much fewer interesting and high-ranking positions available for foreign nationals in an MNC. If, for example, regional headquarters are established so as to have substantive roles and functions, it might prove much more interesting for ambitious people with talent. Regional headquarters also make career path planning a lot easier. For example, one Japanese consumer electronics company sends a young accountant to Malaysia as an apprentice, later transfers her to Indonesia as a manager, and finally promotes her to an executive position in Southeast Asia regional headquarters. Likewise, a Chinese section manager in Taiwan may be promoted to division manager in Hong Kong, and eventually become country manager in Singapore. Of the American companies, Citicorp appears to be the most advanced in this area. It is quite deeply involved in the local financial scene everywhere I have been to in Asia, including Japan. Its career path planning appears to be quite cosmopolitan.

Degree of Localization

Since the presence of regional headquarters is a matter of strategic and operational convenience, its use should not be carried too far so as to become an extra layer of control and/or a bureaucratic nuisance.

The design of the ideal global organization should reflect how universal a company's product can be. For example, a product such as a word processor depends heavily on the local language, and hence must be developed to respond to the local needs. There is no use developing an English language word processor and trying to sell it in Japan, except for a specialized use by foreign-affiliated companies. A rice cooker also would be used in countries like Japan, China, and Thailand. However, the Japanese prefer sticky steamed rice, whereas the Chinese prefer a rather dry variety. Understanding these local nuances becomes a key factor for success.

Such products as furniture and refrigerators are heavily influenced by the physical limitations of living space. Normally the modifications needed for tailoring these products to local tastes are major. American-sized furniture would be too big for a typical Japanese or European household. Since most Japanese sleep on the floor, refrigerators must be rather quiet and the hot air from the compressor should not blow from the bottom onto the sleeper's face. Such a consideration probably is not even needed in the United States and Europe where people sleep on elevated beds.

On the other hand, Japanese and European customers prefer a miniature-size component stereophonic set. However, this type of product does not do well in the United States, where physically large speakers and amplifiers are still considered to be prestigious. Americans also prefer an over-sized cabinet-style television to be placed on the floor. However, the Japanese, who normally sit within six feet of the TV set, wouldn't touch such a product because of its poor resolution with current 550 raster technology. As the new 1,000 raster technology becomes more commonplace, we will see larger screens penetrate rather rapidly in Japan. Over the last decade, the average floor space of a kitchen in Japan has increased by 60 percent, and as a result larger refrigerators of over 200 liters have become commonplace.

These are the examples of new opportunities emerging, as the pattern of life in a region shifts. Most American white goods companies came to Japan 10 to 15 years ago when American products were either too big or too powerful. With the emergence of the Triad's universal users, there are much more commonalities in the users' basic product/service preferences. It is a pity that many American and European companies have given up their efforts in Japan too soon to capitalize on their traditional strengths and home-market experiences.

For products like component stereophonic equipment, the basic needs among the Triad customers are almost identical. However, it is also true that Germans like to see color panels with symbols. Particularly after the Munich Olympics, Europeans have started using symbols rather than words on key street signs, toilets, automobile dashboards, and audio panels. For example, "?" means information booth, or the place to ask questions, ◀◀ means rapid rewind, and *P* means a parking lot. Therefore, the leading-edge Japanese consumer electronics companies send their product-design engineers around the world for about six months a year to learn the latest customer needs and survey competitive scenes. They visit customers and dealers, as well as national sales companies, and hold regional product conferences.

These companies shoot for the maximum number of commonalities in design, and then try to be responsive to local tastes, such as symbol panels for Germany and larger-size cabinets for the United States. However different the products may look from the outside, their basic modules, circuits, and concepts are identical; hence, they typically have over 80 percent of manufacturing features in common. This gives the company a true "scale economy" and hence, competitive cost advantage. These products must reflect the differences in the local electric frequencies and voltages and, in the case of color television, differences in technology such as the PAL system in Europe.

However, there is a series of products for which you do not even have to consider these infrastructural differences. For example, products that run on dry cell batteries, like cameras, watches, radios, cassette players, and Walkmans, can be made truly universal. Motorcycles and pianos are also independent of the infrastructural constraints. In these categories, product designers, having spent six months traveling around the world, can sit down at their home offices and reflect on the fresh memories of their Triad trip, and can use their imagination to find what might have the most universal appeal to the Triad's 600 million universal users. Canon's AE-1 single-lens reflex camera and Konica's auto-focus and built-in flash lens–shutter cameras are good examples of products designed from such an approach.

Because of the universality of the users, it could very well happen that detailed attention to a certain group of the people in one given region might also result in a universal product. For example, by observing California's youngsters on rollerskates, a Sony engineer came up with the concept of the Walkman, a portable cassette player. By studying American youths carrying heavy portable radios, a Japanese consumer electronics company came up with a radio-cassette player with extravagant looks and colorful design. Both of these products have found far wider acceptance around the world than the original target customer segment.

Exhibit 12–3 summarizes some personal observations of mine. Here, I have tried to differentiate the functions that must be performed and perfected locally from those which could very well be shared on a global basis. I strongly encourage companies to use this kind of framework to understand a product's degree of universality, particularly on several key functions.

The role assigned to headquarters, regional, and local management should be changed, depending on the results of your analysis of the degree of universality throughout the world by functions. Exhibit 12–4 illustrates this point. For example, if your product requires complete localization in design and marketing functions, then the role of the company management in that country would be greater. On the other hand, if the product can be designed as a universal one on a global scale, then the world headquarters' roles could increase in such functions as R&D, product development, and even production.

These illustrations are all schematic, and simply attempt to highlight what kinds of factors need to be considered. As such, they should not be interpreted as definitive, quantitative recommendations on how to divide labor among country, region, and global headquarters.

After all, any corporation is a product of a company's history, and "the way we do business around here" has a lot to do with the mental and strategic stability of the company. My point here is simply that you should take a fresh look at the existing division of labor, and challenge the status quo and the traditional modus operandi. I do not intend to recommend how far and how fast you should change. That should be carefully studied by the decision-makers and the implementors on a case-by-case basis.

191

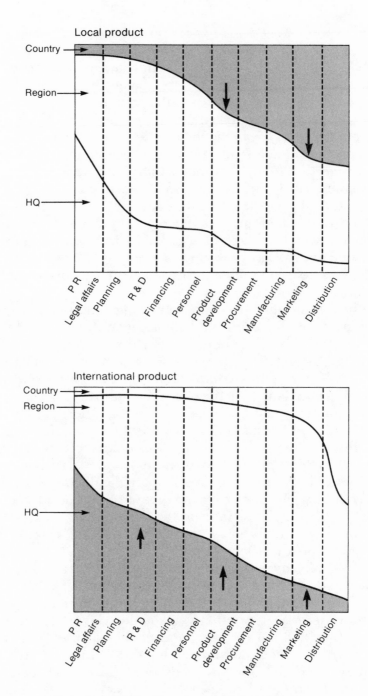

EXHIBIT 12–3   Local and global functions.

Local ← ———————————————————————— → Universal

Factors limiting universality	Culture/ habits	Design taste	Language	Size/package	Technical system	User/ application	None
Example	• Fish sausage • Root beer • Boxer shorts • Rice cooker	• Furniture • Refrigerator • Processed food	• Word processor • Computer	• Textile • Automobile (seat size) • Soft drinks	• Color TV (PAL system in European voltage)	• Portable radio/cassette player (youths in U.S.) • White liqueur (young females in Japan)	• Watch • Motorcycle • Petrochemical products • Piano • Money (capital market)

Key functions:
- Marketing concept
- Technology
- Product application
- Product concept

☐ Must modify locally ▨ Could be shared globally

EXHIBIT 12-4 Degree of universality of product.

Role of Global Headquarters

As we have just seen, the roles of the regional and local companies change depending on the universality of the product or service of a particular company. The role of the global headquarters should also be adjusted accordingly.

However, as we move toward the Triad position, there are definitely several roles that the world headquarters must play uniquely.

Value-Setter

A corporation is like a human being. Without aspirations, objectives, and goals, it tends to live a mundane daily life. As a result, it tends to become a mediocre company without achieving anything new, year in, year out. It will become a "vegetable" company.

The difficulty for a global corporation, however, is to set a universal value system which will work in different countries and regions. Very few companies do this well. Fortunately, however, if you concentrate on the emerging commonalities across the Triad, this task can become a lot easier.

Our firm, McKinsey, has not yet encountered major difficulties in the OECD countries by applying what were originally our North American creeds: "client interest first" and a "top-management perspective" in consulting. Our aspiration to deliver lasting impact on major issues for major institutions has been the key factor in our success in recruiting top-quality staff members in each of the 14 countries we have entered.

Canon changed its corporate value system about ten years ago, from a technology-based consumer opto-electronics company to a "first class" orientation. This has forced the company to compete on an own-brand, as opposed to original equipment manufacturer (OEM), basis in high-quality segments in OECD countries. The strategy has probably weakened the company's position in the developing countries, but has certainly helped the company establish a premier position in

194

camera and plain paper copiers in each of Triad regions. Canon's competitors, such as Ricoh and Mita, enhanced their positions in developing countries, but they remain behind Canon in the key Triad markets. Ryusaburo Kaku, Canon's CEO since 1971, was the value setter. His global perspective and "first class" orientation have permeated throughout its global corporate value system.

If a corporation is a conglomerate or too diversified to have a universal value system, then my suggestion would be to establish two kinds of global value systems. One has something to do with the corporation's quality and aspirations, universally shared regardless of its kind of business. It will be a value shared by all who use the same company insignia. The other set of value systems may be set for a group of businesses with functional commonalities and/or common global competitors.

Take General Electric, for example. It could be divided into such sectorial groups as power generation, consumer appliances and components, each of which has different key factors for success, and each "sector" could have a different (but very focused and effective) value system. Their corporate aspiration of an innovative "general" electric company based on Thomas Edison's founding principles does not necessarily have to conflict with another set of value systems for a specific sector.

Lubricator

Unfortunately, most world headquarters act as a hindrance to the mobility of corporate resources, for example, money, people, and technology. This is largely due to the fact that their own image of what they do is still based on the old corporate model of "plan and control" and/or "divide and govern." This model assumes that the headquarters is inherently in conflict with the regional and national operations. Such an antagonistic model is completely obsolete due to the emergence of the Triad's common customers and competitors.

As such, the need for the global headquarters to control is less, but it has to proactively shift resources from one region to another, depending on the corporation's strategic needs for strengthening certain regions.

As the corporation becomes more of an "insider" in different Triad regions, headquarters' "real" knowledge and such experience as sales-force management, logistics, production planning, and inventory management become important. Such functions are performed well by the home country management with a long, established history. It is, however, often the case that such management systems and experiences do not travel well, and many global corporations' overseas operations are frequently grossly undernourished.

A few years ago, I was invited by a U.S. manager of a Japanese chemical company to examine and diagnose his operations. I found out that he had no systems to keep track of his costs, inventories, receivables, and payables. He had rough estimates of what they were, but was suffering from the lack of any sensible information on company economics. His hiring practice was laissez-faire, and career development programs were nonexistent. His marketing tactics were concentrated on heavy discounting channels because, he said, his boss in Tokyo "did not allow me to develop strategies, and pushed me for volume."

After a quick diagnostic round, I exclaimed, "My goodness! This doesn't look like a company. You should at least ask your Tokyo headquarters guys to come in and have them install the basic infrastructure before you start your operations here!" He replied, "Look, I am the fifth general manager here. If we were sensible at all, the first guy would have done it. The trouble is, since I am the fifth generation, everyone at home thinks we have a company here, and doesn't even give me an accountant. So I had to hire a local one, and naturally, this one doesn't know our company and the way our systems work. So I told him to go ahead and build our own system. Sure, it's imperfect, but I can at least tell if we are selling below our costs!"

Building an "insider" position for overseas operations in

key countries is like building a new company. One would get awfully concerned about "modernizing the management systems" if the subject under analysis were a dynamic new independent company entering the threshold stage where it had to make a transition from the status of a one-person outfit to that of an institution. You need the same degree of attention in building the infrastructure of overseas subsidiaries. Perhaps it requires *more* attention, because such geographically and culturally dispersed subsidiaries will have to be integrated through management systems into a global whole.

What this means is that, while the local management system must have enough flexibility to adapt to specific local conditions, such as hiring and payment practices, the local system has to form part of a harmonious whole on the global scale. If accounting and personnel policies are different from one region to another, it will be virtually impossible to have a coherent global enterprise. For the corporate culture (or, should I say, corporate physiology?) is normally shaped in accordance with the management processes. The behavior of different managers is reflective of what the accounting system is implicitly telling them, and what the personnel system is tacitly encouraging or punishing them for.

For example, if you have an accounting system in which division managers are charged a high interest rate for borrowing from the corporate headquarters, they would become extremely mindful of the total amount of cash requirements and would start acting like heads of small enterprises. Furthermore, if the accounting system is such that a divisional loss or profit is "remembered" over a certain period, then managers will not make daring decisions and careless mistakes. The company eventually is run by "cautious and deep thinkers."

On the other hand, if the management system is such that the divisional loss is "cleared" after consolidation with the rest of the corporation every year, and managers are allowed to start their books afresh every year, then managers will become quite bold and risk-taking. However, they will also start showing signs of irresponsibility and lack of deep

197

thinking. The company starts to dig a few big holes for itself and becomes rather unstable.

I have seen many accounting systems and personnel policies. It is amazing how many philosophically different systems there are around the world, and yet they are often totally unnoticed by the users themselves. I can almost guess the culture of a corporation rather accurately if I look at these management systems.

Middle managers, or the real shapers of a corporation's corporate culture, do not have the benefit of the teachings and preachings of the CEO every day. But they have to live with the consequences of the management systems day in, day out.

Over time, if what a corporation's top management is saying is in conflict with what its management systems are implicitly imposing, for example, "Be creative, damn it!," then that corporation is in real competition with its own internal management systems. In other words, the corporation's system can undermine the creative potential of the organization. As such, I believe it is quite important to coordinate the shaping of local divisions' basic values and operating philosophy with those of the central corporation, through careful matching of various management systems and processes around the world.

There are only two ways to accomplish this: one is to send enough corporate staff to overseas operations so as to install and instill the infrastructure in them. The other is to hire managers locally, and have them come to the home office, or to a rather well-established and large operation in a foreign country, for a long time to fully absorb the spirit and workings of the management system. Later, these local hires would be transferred back to their own country.

Too many companies skip these time-consuming exercises designed to match the corporate spirit to the management processes. And the result is a constant patchwork. One of the biggest (and typical) hindrances in such a move is headquarters' staff mentality and attitudes. Most corporate staff members have grown up with the domestic company, and as such, have a strong inclination toward getting involved with the (often larger and closer) domestic operations. As a defense against this inclination, overseas divisions themselves often start building up their own staff. Such a buildup may solve the deployment problems, but it will present serious problems in the corporation's efforts to create "cousins" in remote locations.

Exhibit 12–5 is an illustrative sketch of a Japanese multina-

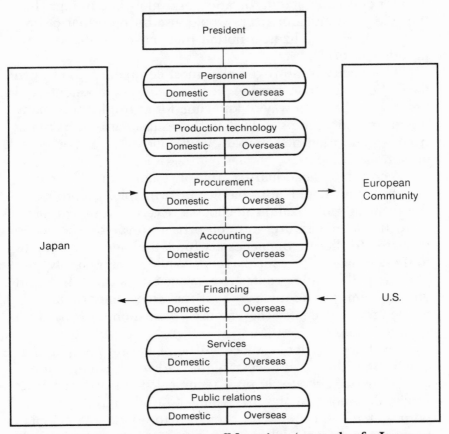

EXHIBIT 12–5 Headquarters staff functions (example of a Japanese electronics company). Headquarters staff functions are to act as transfer agents of "domestic" resources (for example, managers, skills, money) to critical overseas regions.

tional's solution to such a problem. In essence, this company redefined all headquarters' staff functions as formally responsible for the global operations, and positioned their explicit role so as to shift human resources out of Japan to the United States and Europe. This redistribution of personnel is not a control function, but a lubricator and facilitator role, and one that is certainly different from many traditionally organized multinational enterprises. On top of these assignments, if you ask, say, the procurement division to coordinate product and components-code standardization and global sourcing, then the role of the headquarters would also become that of low-cost resource mobilizer, a notion that makes strategic sense in today's world.

The reality is, however, that most companies don't even have the same code number for the same component, and hence they have no way of knowing, for example, how many integrated microchips and relays their subsidiaries are buying from Nippon Electric Company and Honeywell, respectively, on a global scale.

A corporate headquarter's role of resource mobilizer and/or lubricator should not change, in principle, according to the form of globalization it chooses. Even if your company takes the joint venture and consortia routes, you should be prepared to allocate the necessary funds and human resources to the ventures with your partners. While it is absolutely true that these alternative routes to on-your-own approach should end up saving some management resources, they should not be designed to choke the resource allocation process from the beginning.

As stated earlier, a successful joint venture requires as much commitment as necessary to build your own operations on the greenfield site. Even a technical tie-up will not bear fruit unless both parties are willing to exchange people, experiment together, and be prepared to admit lots of "nice tries." Headquarters' role as a lubricator is exactly what it says. It should lubricate the implementation of such strategic scenarios as consortia and/or joint ventures, rather than sit and wait for results to come in from the four corners of the world.

200

Strategic Sensitizer

If you are in the office automation industry, you had better be in California or Japan so that you can feel the "breathing" of the industry. If you are a semiconductor manufacturer, you need to visit Hamilton, a large microchip distributor in the United States, or Kyushu, Japan's "silicon island," in order to feel the vibration of the industry. These are the places where trends are visible and widely talked about. Like Milan and, increasingly, Harajuku and Aoyama in Tokyo, in the world fashion industry, insiders residing in the "sensitive zones" can pick up the signals way ahead of their competitors who reside elsewhere. Inhabitants of the Triad, therefore, could have picked up such critical signals as the subtle moves of the Japanese sewing machine companies entering into electronic typewriters, or Sumitomo and Furukawa Copper Wire Works getting into fiber optics.

If you are a true insider and an unbiased resident of the Triad, you would be able to extract the strategic essence from these "sensitive zones" on behalf of the rest of the Triad. Just being a resident of New York does not mean you really know what's going on in the Big Apple. Likewise, living in Tokyo's Gaijin district (for example, in Azabu and Roppongi) does not necessarily mean that you will pick up trends in robotics and semiconductors in Japan. You have to become an insider. "Insiders" spend time with the right people, so key information naturally comes to them.

The strategic sensitizer role of a global company's headquarters is such that it picks up critical information in one region, and preempts the opportunities of other companies in other regions. Or, it picks up signals of a structural change in consumers' desires, and comes up with new concepts of product and/or services. In one of the Triad locations, global corporate headquarters can identify a dynamic entrepreneur whose business visions are powerful and universal. Thus, it could enter into a joint venture negotiation with this individual on a global scale well before domestic and global competitors even learn of the entrepreneur. In short, a global headquarters that is a strategic sensitizer acts so as to maximize the corporate wealth by finding opportunities and eliminating blind spots over the entire Triad and its submarkets.

Divisional Coordinator

Last of the critical roles to be played by the global headquarters is to supplement shortcomings in the company's mission and definition in existing operating divisions. This role could also be called a strategic supplementer, in that global headquarters tries to view the world from the standpoint of emerging business opportunities. Most existing business units are defined in a traditional sense.

However, companies have to enlarge their definitions of their businesses. A company divided into a radio division and tape recorder division may miss a new opportunity in opening a radio-cassette division. A company with a television division and a stereophonic division may both miss a new opportunity to make audiovisual information systems, systems in which the color television screen is only an image output terminal for such diverse products as televisions, videocassette recorders (VCRs), video disks, and videotext and home shopping or banking units. The "preamplifier" role of hardware in the age of audiovisual information on systems must change, so that the hardware can act as a control tower for all kinds of audio, video, and information signals.

Today, there is no audio equipment company in which the division making amplifiers has in mind the future audiovisual information systems, and hence is involved in aggressively designing such a control tower so it can perform a variety of functions. As a result, users have to buy all kinds of adaptors in order to make use of new disks, VCRs, videotext devices, and personal computers. I proposed such a system in 1979 to one of Japan's leading electronics companies, and it was only in 1983 that the company was able to come up with a system that was a close approximation of what I depicted. Many times, an operating division's preoccupation with its existing business becomes a major hindrance to capturing and shaping new businesses. Headquarters' function should be to make up for such natural shortcomings and, with vision and imagination, to plant the seeds of future divisions inside the corporation and cooperative efforts outside.

Quite often, when I am involved in assisting a joint venture or a consortia negotiation, the corporation in question does not have the right operating unit for the other company to negotiate with. For example, in a recent negotiation between a Japanese robot manufacturer and an American machine tools maker, neither party had a division with a lot of application engineers. However, the possible area of cooperation was in flexible manufacturing cells, for which the Japanese company would provide the handling robots and the American company would provide the machine tools. Both companies' strengths were hardware oriented. Both companies had the relevant strengths to form a joint venture to market the cells in both Japan and the United States. However, neither company had a general manager imaginative enough to sketch out what was required of the field sales and service forces, which had to include a sizable number of application engineers.

Predictably, the Japanese division manager said she could buy a similar machine tool from another Japanese company and could put the whole thing together on her own. On the other hand, the American manager pulled my sleeve after the negotiations, and told me that his division was actually the first in the world to have produced such a materials-handling robot, which was later discontinued for economic reasons. Hence, given a few years, he could manufacture the whole unit on his own. However, the fact was that both companies were losing their positions in their respective areas, and unless they did something new, both divisions would be struggling just to survive.

In a situation like this, if the headquarters staff had the imagination to see these new needs and had proposed to jointly develop the necessary force of applications engineers anew, the venture would have worked out fine. However, left alone to the heads of both companies' hardware-oriented operating divisions, the discussion did not even get started.

Not many joint ventures and consortia are ready-made. A lot of shortcomings must be corrected. Such initiatives do not normally come from bottom-line-conscious operating divisions. That is why this division coordinator role of the global headquarters is a critical one in forcefully shaping the Triad power for tomorrow.

Insiderization

I have met with many Americans who insisted that Sony was an American company. Akio Morita, one of Sony's founders and the first president of its U.S. operation, would be extremely happy to hear these assertions. Thirty years ago, when I was a schoolboy, one of my relatives had a Renault. I thought it was a Japanese car because the rear-engine French car was one of the most popular models in Tokyo at that time. My two sons, at age ten and five years, can't tell the difference between the national origins of Nestle, Coca-Cola, Knorr, Kodak, Nivea, Pampers, and Johnson's Wax and those of Morinaga, Kirin, Ajinomoto, Kao, and Lion.

These are the names and brands you grow up with. There is nothing foreign in the sound of Schick, Sprite, Mister Donut, Scotties, and Kleenex in Japan today. Or, should I say, there is enough foreignness in such Japanese products sold in Japan as Casio, Canon, Sharp, Toyota, and Seiko. The reality is that people don't really care. So long as it is a good product that meets your needs and tastes and has been around long enough to join the ranks of Hershey candy bars and Wrigley's chewing gum, people don't really care about its origins.

Despite governmental and journalistic antagonisms, the consumers of the world are clearly becoming universal users, or OECD-ites. That is the reason why there are more insiders than generally perceived. Even in industrial products, we are witnessing the same phenomenon. Yoshida Kogyo Kabushiki Kaisha (YKK) in fasteners and zippers, Nihon Gaishi Kabushiki Kaisha in high-voltage insulators, Kyocera in ceramic condensers and packages, and Fujitsu Fanuc in numerical controls all have greater than a 50 percent share of their respective markets in the world.

Just as successful Japanese companies have obtained a high share in their markets, so have Americans in Japan either directly or through joint ventures.

Likewise, joint ventures including American partners in Japan such as Yamatake–Honeywell, Caterpillar–Mitsubishi, Sumitomo–Minnesota Mining and Manufacturing (3M), and Fuji–Xerox are all ranked among the top three in their respective industries. Ebara–Infilco, which was owned by Westinghouse's Infilco Division until recently, is the biggest firm in the Japanese water treatment industry. This is doubly astonishing because more than 90 percent of this company's work was in the public sector, which is notoriously exclusive of outsiders—including the "outsiders" of the Japanese. Similar acclaim goes to the French companies of Schlumberger and Michelin in the United States.

Another cosmopolitan French company, L'Air Liquid, owns 64.2 percent of Teisan, which is publicly traded on the Tokyo Stock Exchange. In fact, the foreign ownership of Japanese corporations is increasing very rapidly. In 1981, there were only three companies listed on the Tokyo exchange that had more than 20 percent of their shares held by foreigners. However, the number shot up to 38 in late 1983. Nobody would have guessed a few years ago that the liberalization of capital participation by foreigners into the mainstream Japanese corporations would be so fast. Five years ago, the capital-markets liberalization and ownership were emotional debates in Japan. Today, foreigners own more than 20 percent of 38 companies and nobody even makes a fuss about it.

All of this evidence verifies the assertions I have been putting forward throughout this book. The Triad is being shaped. It's not a speculation. It is a reality. This reality is blurred by the neoprotectionist overtones reported in every day's news and the emotional and hysterical perspectives promoted by voter-sensitive politicians and excuse-seeking corporate executives.

A Triad power is a corporation that could have a small

corporate center in a place symbolically named "Anchorage," but with a strong insider position in Japan, the United States, and the European Community, as well perhaps as one or two other critical regions depending on its historical and strategic needs. Its insider positions in these regions are testified to by the following characteristics:

1. Well-established management systems

2. Full set of business functions spontaneously responsive to local conditions (though they may be supplemented by headquarters' and other regions' functions where it makes strategic sense)

3. Management fully familiar with local and regional customers and competitors

4. Continuity in management, with mostly home-grown and globally trained personnel

5. Quick and autonomous decision-making, but which is fully synchronized and in communication with the rest of the corporation (that is, corporate headquarters is fully informed of, but seldom interferes with, regional management)

6. Strong "staying power" during periods of discontinuity and difficulty in the key markets, with creative solutions which respond to changing markets

7. Active communications at all costs within the corporation at the interfaces with affiliated companies, and with the headquarters, by telephone and face-to-face conversations as well as by longer-term exchange of people

8. Little tolerance for standard "it's-out-of-my-control" excuses regarding shortcomings and mistakes

9. Significant presence and weight felt throughout the community where operations are located.

These are the characteristics of true insiders. They behave so naturally it would be difficult to distinguish them from incumbents. In fact, being a Triad power is nothing but being an "honorable incumbent." It is in this context that I have suggested two routes by which a firm may become a Triad power, other than on its own. If the corporation's own judgment is that it is excessively difficult to fully meet the nine conditions listed above, then my recommendation would be to seriously consider a form of partnership, such as joint ventures and/or consortia formation. In doing so, the joint venture route has the difficulty of matching two different corporate cultures through rather unnatural legal contracts. Ownership and who's-got-control issues also come in, which are fundamentally incompatible with the notion of "doing business" pragmatism and entrepreneurship.

Unless the corporation is fully prepared to match the culture of its partner or maintain the original spirit of the joint venture without recourse to the contract, the joint venture's long-term viability is questionable. Consortium formation tends to be viewed as a matter of tactical convenience. However, I do not think so. Given the company's difficulties in penetrating into the major Triad markets on its own, and given the difficulties of creating and modifying the traditional corporate culture in order to establish an insider position in any part of the Triad, it is my conviction that a consortium consisting of true insiders in the respective key regions would enable each member company to enjoy almost an instant access to a large number of relevant customers. It would also give each of the member companies insight into the purchasing, manufacturing, marketing, distribution, personnel, and financing aspects of operating in tough but lucrative Triad markets.

Traditional multinationals have tried to do everything on their own as they entered each market. They can't do that anymore because the skills and products required to compete worldwide have increased greatly. My point has been that this need not be the case; corporations don't have to be confined by their individual limits if they learn how to form consortia. The future key factor for success for multinationals will be their ability to develop and enhance company-to-company relationships, particularly across national and cultural boundaries.

Any corporation entering into a consortium arrangement, however, will have to keep in mind two points:

1. It will have to allow positive, proactive, and strategic interlinkages across all participating companies, instead of using cautious, suspicious, and distant alliances of convenience. This may not be possible at the beginning, but the corporation will, at least, have to allow the hope of doing so in the long run.

2. The corporation must be prepared to gradually adjust its business system and language so that consortium members can minimize friction in communicating and agreeing on critical matters. This change will have to occur so as to keep smooth communication among partners at all levels of management and at all times.

I wanted to stress in this book that a corporation must be prepared to change its value systems and culture, to honestly face up to the realities of the competition and customers in the Triad.

Old frameworks designed for, at the most, 200 million people, have become obsolete in the Triad's new and dynamic markets of 600 million people. The consumer behavior of the Triad's residents is becoming remarkably similar. In the same way, industrial goods such as machine tools and control instruments are not so different in terms of the users' basic needs across the Triad. But neither consumer nor industrial customers can be captured at a single sweep, by the use of a monolithic approach and a single business system around the world. Universal users encourage global enterprises to do business in all parts of the Triad. At the same time, given the differences in business practice and in the local infrastructure of distribution, personnel, production, and engineering, and given the unfortunate political pressures of protectionism, a company must establish a true insider position in each of the key Triad regions.

In accordance with this new reality and perspective, a corporation must be prepared to change its traditional culture and value system to transform itself into a new global power, into a Triad power, with a significantly different chemistry and blood type.

Let me try to state the key messages of this book succinctly:

△ *Learn to work with others.* The key to success for corporations competing on a global scale will be their ability to develop the skills necessary to interact with other equally prestigious corporations without having unproductive hiccups and nervous breakdowns.

△ *Build your business on similarities.* Both in business and in politics, we have all stressed differences of culture and nationalities. And yet the emergence of global needs makes it clear that a corporation can build its business and product/service concept on the similarities among 600 million Triadians in consumer goods, or on similarities in modus operandi in industrial goods.

△ *Commit, I mean, really commit yourself to a global perspective.* Overseas business cannot be the antithesis of domestic business. In order to establish a truly global business, companies must view the world from a global perspective. People, systems, and organizational structure all must reflect this perspective. Unless organized correctly, the corporation will not become a true Triad power. This means that instead of an opportunistic approach to generating business worldwide, you really have to *commit* your firm to the building of a global corporate infrastructure from the beginning. Domestic operations can be only a part of the global whole.

In a world growing closer and more complex, where competition is becoming more intense yet more cooperative, the customer more universal yet more distinct, the successful organization will be both more independent and more interdependent.

NOTES

Chapter 2. The Accelerating Tempo of Technology

1. *Automobile Industry Handbook*, Research Department, Nissan Motor Co., 1984.
2. Ibid.
3. *Appliance Manufacturer*, Cahners Publishing Co., Boston, January 1983, p. 65.
4. *Japan Market Share Yearbook*, Yano Research Institute, Tokyo, 1984.
5. *Financial Times*, May 30, 1984.

Chapter 3. The Universal Users

1. *International Statistical Yearbook, 1983*, The Prime Minister's Office of Japan.
2. Ibid.
3. Ibid.
4. *Statistical Yearbook, 1983*, UNESCO.
5. Ibid.
6. *International Statistical Yearbook, 1983*, Research Department, Bank of Japan.

Chapter 5. Global Impasse

1. Telephone interview, Japan Safety Razor Industrial Association, August 1984.
2. *Automobile Industry Handbook*, Research Department, Nissan Motor Co., 1984.
3. Ibid.
4. Ibid.
5. Ibid.
6. Public Relations Department, Honda Motor Co., August 1984.
7. Ibid.
8. *Automobile Industry Handbook*, Research Department, Nissan Motor Co., 1984.
9. Ibid.
10. *Automobile Industry Handbook*, Research Department, Nissan Motor Co., 1982.
11. Ibid.
12. *Automobile Industry Handbook*, Research Department, Nissan Motor Co., 1984.
13. *Annual Corporation Reports, (Unlisted)*, Nikkei Co., 1984.
14. *Japan Market Share Yearbook*, Yano Research Institute, Tokyo, 1984.
15. Ibid.
16. *Appliance Manufacturer*, Cahners Publishing Co., Boston, January 1983, p. 65.
17. Ibid.
18. Public Relations Department, Matsushita Electric Industrial, August 1984.
19. *Japan Market Share Yearbook*, Yano Research Institute, Tokyo, 1984.
20. *Appliance Manufacturer*, Cahners Publishing Co., Boston, January 1983, p. 65.
21. Op. cit.
22. Op. cit.
23. *Mintel*, January 1983, p. 41.

Chapter 6. True Competitors

1. *Automobile Industry Handbook*, Research Department, Nissan Motor Co., 1984.
2. *Nikkei Industrial Paper*, May 14, 1984, p. 20.
3. *Japan Market Share Yearbook*, Yano Research Institute, Tokyo, 1974, 1976, 1978.

4. *Japan Market Share Yearbook,* Yano Research Institute, Tokyo, 1980, 1982, 1984.
5. The following Honda–Yamaha material has been adapted from "The Honda–Yamaha Battle," *Nekkei Business,* June 13, 1983.
6. *Japan Market Share Yearbook,* Yano Research Institute, Tokyo, 1984.

Chapter 7. Japanese Companies in the United States and Europe

1. *Japan Exports & Imports,* Japan Tariff Association, December 1983.
2. *Japan Market Share Yearbook,* Yano Research Institute, Tokyo, 1984.
3. Telephone interview, Japan Industrial Sewing Machine Association, August 1984.
4. Telephone interview, Japan Camera Industry Association, August 1984.
5. Ryuji Yasuda, doctoral thesis, University of California, Berkeley, 1978.
6. Public Relations Department, Sony Corp., August 1984.
7. Public Relations Department, Honda Motor Co., August 1984.
8. *Nikkei Paper,* December 18, 1984, p. 9.
9. *Annual Foreign Corporation Reports,* Nikkei Co., 1984.

Chapter 8. U.S. and European Companies in Japan

1. U.S. Department of Commerce, 1984.

Chapter 9. Emergence of the Triad

1. *Japan Economic Journal,* August 1, 1984.
2. *Japan Economic Journal,* February 19, 1984.
3. *Managing the International Company: Building a Global Perspective,* The Conference Board, 1982.

Chapter 12. The Road to Becoming a Triad Power

1. Setsutaro Kobayashi, *Watashino Rirekisho* [My Personal History], published by *Japan Economic Journal,* 1981.

GLOSSARY

Abbreviation	Full Spelling and Meaning
ASEAN	Association of Southeast Asian Nations
AVIS*	Audiovisual information system
EC	European Community
JE	Japan–European Community
JU	Japan–United States
JUE	Japan–United States–European Community
LDC	Less-developed country
MLC*	Multilocal company
MNC	Multinational corporation
MNE	Multinational enterprise
MRC*	Multiregional company
NIC	Newly industrialized country (for example, Korea, Taiwan, Mexico, Hong Kong, or Singapore)
OECD	Organization for Economic Cooperation and Development
OECD-ites*	Residents of the OECD
OEM	Original equipment manufacturer; a producer of products on behalf of another company brand name goods
OPEC	Organization of Petroleum Exporting Countries
UE	United States–European Community
UNCTAD	United National Conference on Trade and Development

* Term unique to this book.

INDEX

Index

217